MW01247413

JURAN GLOBAL
Lean & Six Sigma

Reference Guide & Tool Kit

About Juran Global

Juran Global is a US based, internationally-acclaimed, business improvement consulting and training organization founded as Juran Institute in 1979, by Dr. Joseph M. Juran. Dr. Juran was one of the most internationally recognized pioneers and visionaries in attaining business results through the management of quality as viewed by the customer.

The new Juran Global under the leadership of Joseph A. DeFeo M.B.A., Dr. Juran's contemporary, is providing these materials for the global marketplace to assure Dr. Juran's methods are properly presented for maximum results.

Juran Global is available to conduct this workshop at your location, anywhere in the world or through our distant learning programs.

Juran Global offers best-in-class assessment, benchmarking, consulting, and training services to implement operational excellence programs aimed at improving business results. Our services include assessment tools that benchmark against international best practices, and training programs to deploy operational excellence, change management, and quality management.

Contact Juran Global at
tina@juran.com

Juran Global Development Team

Joseph A. De Feo, Editor
Jeremy Hopfer, Project Manager, Copy Editor, Graphics, and Layout
Michelle Matschke, Copy Editor
Thomas DeFeo, Cover Design

Juran Inventory #6025
Copyright © September 2014

ISBN-13: 978-1479357864

ISBN-10: 1479357863

Table of Contents

Table of Contents

Table of Contents

JURAN GLOBAL

Lean &
Six Sigma

Reference Guide & Tool Kit

Introduction to This Guide

This Reference Guide was created to provide practitioners with brief and pertinent information on deploying lean and/or six sigma projects. It contains an explanation of the Lean and Six Sigma methods, important tools, and team skills required to carry-out successful deployment of Lean or Six Sigma.

In addition it contains key information related to important roles, how to select and launch projects, and valuable deployment tips. The information contained in this guide is generic enough for you to adapt to your own needs. Each topic was taken from the Juran Institute, Inc. training materials that have been used by many for over 30 years.

This guide is not meant to be all inclusive. The included tools and techniques combine the best practices recognized to enable your organization to improve performance.

For more information please contact us at
www.juran.com.

The Imperative:
Superior Results

1. Continuously improving quality of goods and services will help attain superior results.
2. Having a systematic approach and program to improve the organization's performance is required.
3. A performance improvement program should focus on both improving process effectiveness with Six Sigma, and process efficiency with Lean.
4. A successfully deployed program will create breakthroughs in performance.
5. Understanding all processes needs to become faster and better, thereby improving performance.
6. Analyzing processes must happen efficiently, quickly, and seamlessly.
7. Using data obtained from a process and turning it into information that will quickly lead to changes will enable your organization to meet its needs of its stakeholders.

What are Lean and Six Sigma?

1. Lean and Six Sigma are two complementary methods that, when combined, will enable an organization to improve continuously improve performance.
2. They focus on understanding your customer needs and then reduce the non-value added process waste which cause customer dissatisfaction and long cycle times.
3. Lean and Six Sigma methods and tools minimize the resources required for delivering your goods, information or services to your customers by eliminating waste that inflates costs, lead times, and inventory.
4. Process improvement happens "project by project." Each project (a problem to solve) is selected by a Champion (a leader); has its own mission (a project charter); a project leader (a Black or Green Belt) and a team of subject matter experts all trained in Lean and Six Sigma.

What is Six Sigma?
The Equation "Y=f(X)"

Six Sigma is about improving what is important or "critical to the customer (CTQs)." We call this the "Y." The equation Y = f(x) is used to guide the team and help communicate what a project is trying to accomplish.

Once we understand what the Ys are we then measure them to see if we are meeting the target. We analyze the Ys to understand the process characteristics that cause variation, and then reduce their variation by controlling the process variables. We call these variables the "Xs." There may be many Xs that can impact the Y.

If Y is a function of X, then all we need to do is define the Xs with enough precision to control them. Once controlled, the Y should be met.

Once this is done we then hold the gains to maintain performance.

$$Y = f(x_1, x_2, x_3, x_4, \ldots)$$

What is Lean?

Lean is a methodology used to perform faster, cheaper, better. It sets out to improve cycle time, throughput, and eliminate common types of process waste.

Lean differs in focus from Six Sigma. It starts with defining value in terms of the benefits the customer gains from the goods or services that are produced. It is conducted in Rapid Improvement or Kaizen events instead of projects.

A lean expert working with subject matter experts attempts to understand the "value streams" (the end to end process tasks that when combined together add value to the good or service produced). They then synchronize processes with customer demand. This enables them to drive out the 8 common wastes in processes:

1. Overproducing
2. Waiting
3. Transport
4. Poor process design
5. Inventory
6. Motion
7. Defects
8. Underutilized personnel and creativity

The Champion's Role

Champions are management representatives who select projects within a business unit, function, or process. Champions are not just from management; they are those who want to demonstrate the benefits of Six Sigma and Lean, and are willing to take a risk to achieve the intended results. Champions are viewed as the leaders of the improvement initiatives and must conduct the activities on the following pages before the team begins the Define Phase.

Top 10 Champion Tasks:
1. Performs a key role in the organization's business strategy to drive down costs and increase revenue and profitability
2. Identifies those to perform in a Black Belt role
3. Nominates, selects, and writes the project charter critical to meeting goals, and chooses the right project leader(s) and team members
4. Understands the use of Lean and Six Sigma tools and techniques
5. Mentors and advises peers on prioritizing, planning, and launching projects
6. Removes organizational obstacles that may impede the work of the project leaders and their teams
7. Provides approval and support to implement remedies to business processes
8. Asks questions to understand if the team is making progress
9. Provides recognition and reward to the project leaders upon successful completion of their projects
10. Communicates with executive management and peers on the progress and results associated with improvement efforts

What is a Project?

A project is a "problem scheduled for a solution" or a process that needs to be improved to meet stakeholder needs.

A Lean or Six Sigma project is different from other 'projects' that take place daily. It is an agreed upon "problem to be solved." In other words it is scheduled for completion. Resources are assigned to it. It has support of leaders and a has a great chance of completion and success.

All improvement happens project by project.

Projects can be large or small in scope and results.

Some projects take longer to complete than others, not because the method used takes too long, but because the project may be very complex.

Lean or Six Sigma can be the method used to complete a project. The Master Black Belt, Black Belt or Green Belt assigned to the project can determine the best tool set depending on the problem statement provided by the Champions.

There is a common set of practices to select useful projects.

How Projects are Nominated

Champions, working with others, align projects to organizational goals. They gather information from organization stakeholders and customers that can be used to nominate and launch projects.

Nominations can come from many sources such as:
- Reviewing customer and stakeholder complaints
- Conducting reviews and audits to gain data on the costs of poor performance and poor scorecard results
- Aligning business plans: Your mission, long-term strategic goals, business plans, or other business objectives not being met
- Completing other projects: Existing projects may be separated into smaller, more manageable projects
- Asking staff: The organization's managers and other employees are often the first to recognize opportunities for improvement – talk to them!

The Champion's role at this point is to create a list of problems and label them "potential" projects. This is not the time to judge or select the projects. The objective is to obtain a comprehensive list.
For each project write a brief one or two line problem statement to describe "what is wrong."

How to Evaluate and Select the Right Projects

Collect specific, objective data on how each identified problem may impact the organization. Some typical areas to collect data:

- Satisfying stakeholders and customers
- Achieving strategic goals
- Reducing costs
- Enhancing employee satisfaction
- Reducing cycle time

Projects are selected using "Must" and "Want" criteria. "Must" criteria are yes/no considerations, and only those projects that contain all of the "Must" criteria should be considered further. The "Must" criteria answer the questions of whether a project is:

- Measurable
- Observable/Chronic
- Manageable/of a Measurable Size
- Significant

Once it is determined that a project has all of the "Must" criteria, it is ranked according to the magnitude of the "Want" criteria:

- Greatest Impact on Focal Points
- Urgency
- Risks
- Potential Resistance to Change

Once this ranking is complete it is time to create a Project Charter.

Create Project Charter

A Project Charter:
- Clarifies what is expected of the project and the team
- Keeps the team focused on the Y
- Keeps the team aligned with organizational priorities
- Helps the team share information about the project
- Transfers the project from the Champion to the team

The Project Charter is a one-page document
that contains the six elements listed below:
1. Problem statement
2. Goal statement
3. Business case/expected benefits
4. Project scope
5. Milestones/project plan
6. Team members/resource roles

What is a Problem Statement?

Prepare the problem statement and assure it is:

Measurable, indicating the scope of the problem in quantifiable terms, such as Defects per Million Opportunities (DPMO)

Observable and Chronic, describing visible evidence of the problem, delays, errors, etc.

Manageable, meaning it can be resolved in a reasonable time frame (three to six months)

Significant, it is worth doing.

An effective problem statement also does not:
- Imply cause
- Assign blame
- Suggest a remedy

What is a Goal Statement?

Write the project team's goal statement.

Base the goal on what the organization wants to accomplish, that is, what the team should do to solve the problem.

Describe the level of improvement the team must achieve i.e., decrease defects from 10 to 1, reduce waste, cost, etc.

The goal statement should be SMART. SMART goal statements should be **S**pecific, **M**easurable, **A**greed Upon, **R**ealistic, and **T**ime-phased. Read more about the SMART method on page 124.

Select Project Leaders and Teams

Effective teams include leaders trained in Lean and Six Sigma as Lean Experts, Black Belts, or Green Belts. Team members are skilled in the methods and tools.

1. Identify employees to support the project that are most closely associated with the problem. Ask:
   a. Where is the problem observed or the pain felt?
   b. Where might sources or causes of the problem be found?
   c. Who has special knowledge, information, or skill in uncovering the root cause of the problem?
   d. What parts of the organization would be helpful in implementing a remedy?
2. Assign the Black Belt and/or Green Belt.
3. Verify that the team has representation from each of the key functions of the organization.
4. Evaluate each team member to assure each has:
   a. Direct, detailed, personal knowledge of some part of the problem or process being improved
   b. Time for team meetings and assignments

Key Roles for Success

Master Black Belt/Lean Master
- Provides technical support and mentoring
- Facilitates multiple projects
- Provides advice to Champions and Executive Management
- Trains others on the Lean and Six Sigma tools and techniques
- Provides leadership to management groups during integration of the Lean and Six Sigma approaches with the organization's business strategy
- Contributes to creating and carrying out the organization's strategic business and operational plans
- Is trained on advanced tools, strategic deployment, and train the trainer workshops

Black Belt/Lean Expert
- Develops, coaches, leads Six Sigma and Lean teams
- Mentors and advises Champions and management on prioritizing, planning, and launching Six Sigma and Lean projects
- Uses Six Sigma and Lean tools and methods to complete projects
- Mentors Green Belts

Green Belt
- Leads a project team of smaller scope or is a team member on a large project
- Uses the Six Sigma and Lean tools and methods to complete projects

Team Member
- Is a team member with a Black Belt or Green Belt team
- Learns the basic Six Sigma and Lean tools and methods to complete projects

Deployment Leader
The Deployment Leader is responsible for the oversight of the performance excellence initiative within the organization. The Leader is responsible for the development, execution, and monitoring of the deployment plan.

Process Owner

A process owner is a business manager with primary responsibility for the ongoing performance of the process being improved. A process owner's key roles include:

- Manages the process to be improved
- Commits to:
    - Helping teams understand the current process
    - Implementing the proven remedies at the Improve Phase
    - Maintaining the process at the Control Phase
- Institutionalizes team-developed procedures, standard work, templates, and tools
- Responsible for "holding the gains"
- Ensures continued incremental improvement
- Maintains all project documentation at the completion of the project

The DMAIC Roadmap

Define
- Develop Project Charter
- Determine Customers & CTQs
- Map High-Level Process

Measure
- Measure Ys
- Plan for Data Collection
- Validate Measurement System
- Measure Baseline Sigma
- Identify Possible Xs

Analyze
- Test Hypotheses
- List Vital Few Xs

Improve
- Select the Solution
- Design the Solution, Controls, & Design for Culture
- Prove Effectiveness

Control
- Identify Control Subjects
- Develop Feedback Loops
- Develop Process Control Plan to Hold the Gains
- Document, Implement, Replicate

Define: Review Project Charter with Team

A Project Charter:
- Clarifies what is expected of the project and the team
- Keeps the team focused on the Y
- Keeps the team aligned with organizational priorities
- Helps the team share information about the project
- Transfers the project from the Champion to the team
- Contains the elements listed below:
    - Problem statement
    - Goal statement
    - Business case/expected benefits
    - Project scope
    - Milestones/project plan
    - Team members/resource roles

Define: Map Process and Determine CTQs

Determine customers and CTQs.
1. List known customers.
2. Gather known customer needs.
3. Translate customer needs into CTQs.

Map the high-level process to:
1. Identify the start and end point of the process
2. Create a SIPOC
3. Create a 2-3 level map
4. Validate process maps
5. Verify customers and CTQs
6. Identify the Ys

Measure: Measure the "Y"

1. Develop operational definitions by defining key terms, i.e., the language the customer uses.
2. Measure the Y: the outward, observable evidence of the problem.
   a. Identify what to measure. Consider:
      - Consistency with problem statement
      - Importance to the customers
   b. Identify units of measure.
      - How do customers measure the Y?
   c. Create sensors to measure the system.
      - What method is most appropriate to measure the Y?
      - Calculate the sigma level for the Y.
3. Define the boundaries. Create a process map or value stream map to better understand the process.
4. Concentrate on the "vital few" by creating a Pareto Analysis. This will help to identify the vital few symptoms of the problem and reminds the team to concentrate solely on them.
5. If any of this modifies the problem or goal statement, it must be reviewed with the Champion.

Measure: Identify Possible Xs

1. Generate a list of potential causes of the Y called Xs or theories.
   a. Have all team members contribute ideas.
2. Organize the theories (Xs) in a cause-effect diagram.
   a. Clarify the theories contributed to ensure that they are understood by all.
   b. Group similar theories.
   c. Ask 'why' five times for each theory.
3. Review the theories.
   a. Check all branches of the cause-effect diagram for logical consistency.
   b. Check each branch for completeness.
   c. Using the process knowledge the team has gained, identify the theories to test their impact on the Y.
4. Determine data-collection method for testing theories.

Analyze: Test Theories

1. Select theories to test.
2. Plan for data collection.
   a. Describe the data required.
   b. Decide where to collect the data.
   c. Decide how to collect the data.
   d. Design the data collection.
   e. Train the data collectors.
3. Collect the data.
4. Analyze the results by deciding:
   a. Which theories are supported by the results
   b. Which theories are eliminated by the results
   c. What new theories are suggested by the results
5. Repeat process as necessary until the root causes are found. Once found, "optimize" the variables to assure your goal is met.

Analyze: Identify Root Cause(s)

1. Re-examine data of any proposed root causes.
   a. Retain the theory if consistent with the data.
   b. Discard the theory if not consistent with the data.
   c. Identify any new theories consistent with all the data.
2. Depending on the initial tests of theories, the team may need to consider additional statistical tests to determine root cause.
3. Conduct hypothesis tests to determine sources of variation and cause and effect relationships among theories tested.
4. Identify the root cause(s). A theory proven to have the greatest impact on the Y, and is able to be controlled, is a root cause of the problem.

Improve: Generate and Evaluate Solutions

1. Identify a broad range of possible solutions.
2. Agree on criteria against which to evaluate the solutions and on the relative weight each criterion will have. The following criteria are commonly used:
   a. Impact on the problem
   b. Total cost
   c. Benefit/cost relationship
   d. Cultural impact/resistance to change
   e. Implementation time
   f. Risk
   g. Health, safety, and the environment
3. Evaluate the solutions using agreed upon criteria.
4. Use a solution matrix or Pugh analysis.
5. Agree on the solution that meets the goal.

Improve: Design the Solution

1. Evaluate the solution and verify that it will meet project goals.
2. Identify customers that will be impacted by a change in process.
    a. Those who will create part of the solution
    b. Those who will operate the revised process
    c. Those served by the solution
3. Determine the required resources to carry out the change.
    a. People
    b. Money
    c. Time
    d. Materials
4. Specify new procedures.
5. Assess human resource requirements, especially training.
6. Verify that the design of the solution meets customer needs.

Improve: Design for Your Culture

1. Identify likely sources of resistance (barriers) and supports (aids) to ensure the solution will be accepted. Resistance typically arises because of:
   a. Unwillingness to change customs
   b. The need to acquire new skills
   c. Unwillingness to adopt a remedy "not invented here"
   d. Failure to recognize that a problem exists
   e. Failure of previous solutions
   f. Belief that it costs too much
2. Rate the barriers and aids according to their perceived impact on the solution.
3. Identify the countermeasures needed to overcome the barriers. Consider the rules of the road:
   a. Providing participation
   b. Providing enough time
   c. Keeping proposals free of excess baggage
   d. Treating people with dignity
   e. Reversing positions
   f. Dealing with resistance seriously and directly

Improve: Prove Effectiveness

1. Decide how the solution will be tested.
   a. Agree on the type of test.
   b. Decide when, how long, and who will conduct the test.
   c. Prepare a test plan.
2. Identify limitations of the test.
3. Develop approach to deal with limitations.
4. Conduct the test.
5. Measure results.
6. Adjust the solution if results are not satisfactory.
7. Retest, measure, and adjust until satisfied that it will work under operating conditions.

Improve: Implement

1. Develop a plan for implementation that indicates:
   a. How, when, and where the remedy will be implemented
   b. Why the change is necessary and what it will achieve
   c. The detailed steps to be followed in the implementation
2. Involve those affected by the change in the planning and implementation.
3. Coordinate changes with the Leadership Team, Champion, Quality Council, project leaders, steering committee, and the affected managers.
4. Ensure preparations are completed before implementation, including:
   a. Written procedures
   b. Training
   c. Equipment, materials, and supplies
   d. Staffing changes
   e. Changes in assignments and responsibilities
5. Monitor the results.

Control: Identify Control Subjects

1. Provide the means to measure the results of the new process.
   a. End-result measures
   b. In-process measures
2. Establish the control standard for each measure.
   a. Base each control standard on the actual performance of the new process.
3. Determine how the actual performance will be compared to the standard.
4. Design actions to regulate performance if it does not meet the standard. Use a control spreadsheet to develop an action plan for each control variable.
5. Establish self-control for individuals.
   a. They know what is expected
   b. They know their actual performance
   c. They are able to regulate the process because they have:
      – A capable process
      – The necessary tools, skills, and knowledge
      – The authority

Control: Mistake Proof the Process

1. Identify the kind(s) of tactic(s) that can be incorporated into the solution to make it mistake proof. Some options include:
   a. Designing systems to reduce the likelihood of error
   b. Using technology rather than human sensory
   c. Using active rather than passive checking
   d. Keeping feedback loops as short as possible
2. Design and incorporate the specific steps to implement mistake proofing into the solution.

Control: Develop Process Control Plan

1. Integrate controls with Balanced Scorecard.
2. Develop systems for reporting results.
    a. When developing systems for reporting results, determine:
        – What measures will be reported, how frequently, and to whom (should be a level of management prepared to monitor progress and respond if gains are not held)
3. Document the controls.
    a. When documenting the controls, indicate:
        – The control standard
        – Measurements of the process
        – Feedback loop responsibilities
4. Team must monitor controls until the goal is met.

Control: Replicate and Nominate New Projects

1. Discuss replication opportunities to translate knowledge from this project to other similar parts of the organization.
2. Identify potential projects. Potential projects may be found by investigating:
   a. The "useful many" possible sources of the original problem
   b. Any previously undocumented deficiencies uncovered by the team
   c. The root cause(s) from other projects to see if they suggest a common, underlying problem
3. Compile a list of potential projects. Provide the list to the Leadership Team, Champion, Black Belt, or Steering Team.
4. Champion signs off that project is complete.

The Lean Roadmap

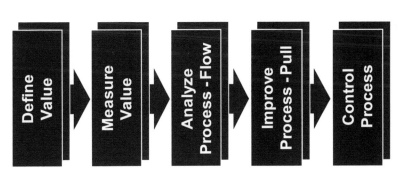

Define Value
- Define Stakeholder Value and CTQs
- Define Customer Demand
- Map High-Level Process
- Assess for 6S Implementation

Measure Value
- Measure Customer Demand
- Plan for Data Collection
- Validate Measurement System
- Create a Value Stream Attribute Map
- Determine Pace, Takt-Time, and Manpower
- Identify Replenishment and Capacity Constraints
- Implement S1 – S3

Analyze Process - Flow
- Analyze the Value Stream Attribute Map
- Analyze the Process Load and Capacity
- Perform VA/NVA Decomposition Analysis
- Apply Lean Problem Solving to Solve Special Causes

Improve Process - Pull
- Conduct the Rapid Improvement Event
- Design the Process Changes and Flow
- Feed, Balance, Load the Process
- Standardize Work Tasks
- Implement New Processes

Control Process
- Stabilize and Refine the Value Stream
- Complete Process and Visual Controls
- Identify Mistake-proofing Opportunities
- Implement S4 – S6
- Monitor Results and Closeout Project

Select a Lean Project

Much like the Six Sigma project pipeline process, Champions identify value streams affecting the strategic objectives and/or goals of the organization during Lean initiatives. They establish projects directly related to those objectives. They define the value stream focus. The results are:

- A list of nominated projects with COPQ and contribution to strategic/business objective(s)
- Selected projects, goal statements for selected projects; Masters, Experts, and teams selected for each project
- Well written problem and goal statements
- Value stream identified for improvements

Define Value

The first step in the Lean roadmap is to Define Value. Its purpose is to validate the value stream improvement focus: problem statement, goal statement, scope of the project and voice of the customer. Like a Six Sigma project, a charter is developed and verified.

Stakeholder value is defined and CTQs are developed.

- List known customers.
- Gather known customer needs.
- Translate customer needs into CTQs.

Define Value: Demand

A SIPOC is developed and customer demand is determined. Demand can be stationary, growth (up or down), or seasonal. Product families are aggregate groupings of similar items/processes/sales items.
Forecasts look at history and customer demand.
Demand is found through:

- Firm orders from all customers for finished products, forms, information, or process result
- Firm orders for service
- Customer forecasts for future orders or demand

Types of demand include:

- Stationary demand – constant over time
- Growth demand – trending upward or downward over time
- Seasonal demand – quantity is influenced by season of year (i.e., air conditioners have high demand in spring and summer)

Define Value: Determining Demand

Lead time and takt time are critical terms to determine demand. Lead time (LT) is the total time it takes to receive, produce, and ship an order. Its elements are:

- LT = Order entry time + Production time + Assembly time + Pick and Pack time + Transit time
- Takt time is the amount of time it takes for a customer to order 1 unit of demand.
    - If you work 8 hours per day and the customer wants 48 items per day takt time is 1/6 hour or 10 minutes per unit.
    - Long lead times inflate inventory and slow customer deliveries. Takt time works to minimize lead time inside a plant and speed orders to customers.

Measure Value

The purpose of the second step in the roadmap is to establish baseline performance for the current process (develop measures that will enable improvement of the performance of the process) to know what to improve.

- Measure customer demand.
- Develop data-collection and sampling plans.
- Create a value stream map.
  - Attributes in the map establish the pace, takt time, and manpower levels.

The team must also identify replenishment and capacity constraints. It is also in this step that the areas involved in the value stream are evaluated for a 5S implementation. If it is determined that 5S is needed, the team would begin by implementing S1 – S3.

Analyze Process - Flow

In the Lean Analyze step, the data and process are examined to determine root causes and opportunities for improvement.

1. Analyze the value stream map.
2. Analyze the process load and capacity.
3. Perform a VA/NVA decomposition analysis.
4. Apply Lean problem solving to solve special causes.

Improve Process - Pull

Like Improve in Six Sigma, improvements are designed and tested in the improve step of Lean. The implementation is through a rapid improvement or Kaizen event. The physical design will accomplish moving from push to pull processes. Process steps are geographically located in cells or lines so that products are made in the same sequence. By making the process steps interdependent, the process is synchronized and bottlenecks are highlighted. This can help remove queues between process steps to reduce cycle time. It can also provide immediate quality feedback. The goal is continuous flow or one piece processing, with minimal setup and changeover times. Strategic inventory is employed in two ways: safety stock compensates for process inefficiencies and buffer stock compensates for customer demand fluctuations. Standard work-in-progress, kanbans, and load charts are employed.

Control Process

The Control step provides the means to measure the revised process on a regular basis, institutionalize the improvement, implement ongoing controls, and sustain the gains. The goal is to stabilize and refine value stream. S4-S6 are completed. Visual controls are set in place, and mistake proofing opportunities are employed.

This page has been intentionally left blank.

JURAN GLOBAL
Lean & Six Sigma

Reference Guide & Tool Kit

Tools

	Lean Six Sigma				
	D	**M**	**A**	**I**	**C**
5-Whys			x		
5S	x	x			x
8 Wastes		x	x	x	
Affinity Diagram and Process	x				
ANOVA			x	x	
Barriers and Aids Chart	x		x	x	
Basic Statistics	x	x	x	x	x
Benefit/Cost Analysis	x			x	
Box Plots		x	x	x	x
Brainstorming	x	x		x	x
Calculating Sigma		x		x	
Cause-Effect Diagram		x	x	x	
Control Chart: p Chart					x
COPQ	x	x		x	
Customer Needs Spreadsheet; VOC	x				
Data Collection	x	x	x	x	x
DOE					
FMEA			x	x	
Fault Tree Analysis			x	x	
Flow Diagram/Process Map			x	x	x
Glossary	x	x			
Graphs and Charts	x	x	x	x	x
Histogram		x	x	x	x
Hypothesis Testing			x	x	x
Kaizen				x	
Kanban				x	
Load Charts			x	x	
MSA		x	x		x
Multi-Vari Charts	x	x	x	x	x

Tools (continued)

	Lean Six Sigma				
	D	M	A	I	C
Pareto Analysis	X	X	X	X	X
Pay-Off Matrix			X	X	
Planning Matrix and Tree Diagram			X	X	X
Planning Network		X	X	X	
Probability			X	X	X	X
Process Capability		X	X	X	
Process Control Plan				X	X
Process Load		X	X	X	
Product Quantity Analysis			X	X	
Product Routing Analysis			X	X	
Pugh Matrix				X	
Push/Pull Systems		X	X	X	
RIE				X	
RCM			X	X	X
Scatter Diagram/Regression Analysis			X	X	X
Sigma Calculation Table	X		X	X	
SMED				X	
SIPOC	X	X			
SMART Method	X				
Solution/Selection Matrix	X			X	
Spaghetti Diagram			X	X	
Standard Work				X	X
Stratification	X	X	X	X	X
Takt Time		X	X		
TPM				X	X
Value Analysis		X			
Value Stream			X		
Value Stream Mapping		X			
Visual Control Boards					X

5-Whys

The 5-whys method focuses on determining the cause of a process failure by repeating the following steps as many times as necessary to uncover the root cause. Five is the suggested number of repeated cycles though some cases may require less and others more.

1. Define the problem or failure.
2. Ask: why did it happen? There are probably multiple possibilities.
3. Go to the location of the problem. Determine which of the possibilities actually caused the problem.
4. Ask: why the item that caused the problem happened? There are probably multiple causes.

Continue steps 3 and 4 until the root cause is identified.

6S

6S is an augmentation of the 5S techniques that were developed in Japan as a way to maintain workplace efficiency and satisfaction. The additional S is for Safety. The objective of 6S implementation is to create a safe and quality workplace using a systematic approach to waste reduction, organization, and housekeeping.

1. Safety: Calls for the implementation of behavioral-based safety processes and procedures that drive zero recordable injuries and zero lost-time accidents. It is the relentless pursuit of "zero" and creating the feeling and substance of a safe work environment.
2. Sort: Fight the human tendency to keep things "just in case."
   a. Decide what is necessary.
   b. Eliminate what is not needed.
   c. Keep only the minimum equipment to support day-to-day operations, get rid of everything that is unnecessary.
   d. Set up a classification system based on the degree of necessity.
3. Straighten: Everything in its place.
   a. Place everything in order and in easy reach.
   b. Install visual controls so that the proper place is obvious, e.g., tool boards.
   c. Create an organized workplace.
   d. Create an inventory system that facilitates access to the tools needed.
   e. Reduce lost time due to walking and searching for tools.
   f. Eliminate lost motion.
4. Shine: Regular cleaning, preventive inspections.
   a. Eliminate trash and dirt.
   b. Make problems easy to spot.
   c. Schedule regular cleaning—everyone participates.
5. Standardize: Establish guidelines.
   a. Establish a system of visual control.
   b. Make the work place easy to maintain by incorporating the first three S's.
6. Sustain: Post results in the workplace.
   a. Make periodic inspections to pre-established guidelines.
   b. Change the culture to promote and permanently maintain a clean and safe workplace.

8 Wastes

Lean identifies and removes unnecessary waste within and around a process. Eight general categories were created to help focus and see the many specific types.

1. **Overproduction**—making or doing more than is required or earlier than needed
2. **Waiting**—for information, materials, people, maintenance, etc.
3. **Transport**—moving people or items around or between sites
4. **Poor process design**—too many/too few steps, non-standardization, inspection rather than prevention, process variation, etc.
5. **Inventory**—supplies, medications, forms, files, finished products, etc.; anything more than the minimum needed to get the job done
6. **Motion**—inefficient layouts at workstations; poor ergonomics in offices; any motion not adding value
7. **Defects**—errors, rework, non-compliance, work-arounds
8. **Underutilized personnel resources and creativity**—ideas that are not listened to, skills that are not utilized

This page has been intentionally left blank.

Affinity Diagrams

Safety Constructed

- No sharp edges
- Won't come apart
- Hard to break
- Non-toxic
- Small pieces won't come off

Holds all Children's Interest

- First toy child picks up
- Uses imagination to create stories
- Used by both girls and boys
- Colorful looking
- Not just a truck

Performance Capabilities

- Motorized
- Can change directions
- Can carry match book type cars

Affinity Diagram and Process

Used when soliciting variable information from customers/employees.

1. Group "like issues."
2. Brainstorm ideas or:
   a. Set a time limit.
   b. Record each idea on adhesive notes or 3x5 cards.
3. Display the ideas on a table or stick them to a wall.
4. Sort into like groups.
   a. Arrange ideas into meaningful categories.
   b. If one idea seems to belong in more than one place, make a duplicate card.
   c. Continue sorting until consensus is reached.
5. Create a title or heading for each category.
6. Transfer the groups to an Affinity Diagram.
7. Reduce the multiple responses to the vital few.

ANOVA

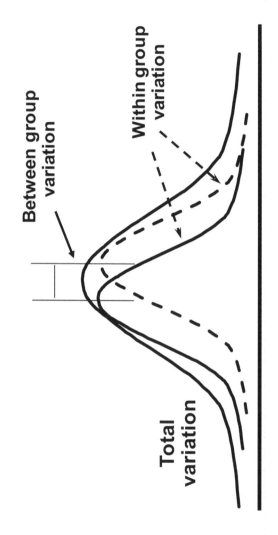

Between group variation

Within group variation

Total variation

ANOVA

Analysis of Variance (ANOVA) is a statistical technique for analyzing data that tests for a difference between multiple (more than two) population means.

The null hypothesis will state that there are no differences among the population means.

H_o: $\mu 1 = \mu 2 = \mu 3$

The alternative hypothesis will specify the following:

H_a: At least one mean is different.

This analysis determines if the differences between the averages of the factor levels are greater than could reasonably be expected from the variation that occurs within the level.

Using ANOVA requires the following:

1. A response that is continuously taken from measurements of the factors sampled.
2. A factor that is categorical with different values (called levels) chosen for the factor.
3. Independent and normally distributed data.
4. Population variances are equal across all levels of the factor.

Barriers & Aids Chart: New Procedure for Engineering Studies

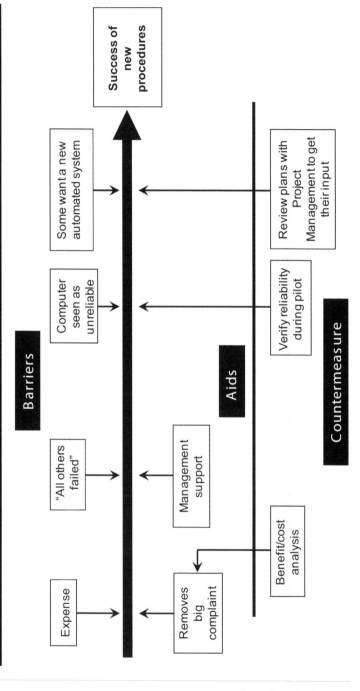

©2014 Juran Institute, Inc.

Barriers and Aids Chart

1. Place a clear description of the objective (remedy) at the far right of the surface being used. Draw a heavy arrow pointing to the objective.
2. Brainstorm a list of potential barriers.
3. Select those vital few barriers that should be overcome, and place them above the heavy arrow labeled as barriers with smaller arrows pointing down.
4. Brainstorm a list of existing aids for overcoming the selected barriers.
5. Select those aids which will help overcome the barriers, and place each one opposite the barrier(s) it will help overcome. Label them as aids.
6. Identify any barriers that will not have adequate aids.
7. Draw a horizontal line below the aids with a "countermeasures" label.
8. Design the countermeasure for barriers without adequate aids, placing them opposite the barriers.
9. Review the chart for missing vital-few barriers, the effectiveness of aids, and the effectiveness of countermeasures.

Basic Statistics

Statistics are necessary to analyze and interpret the data collected on the problem. The two most fundamental concepts in statistical analysis are central tendency and dispersion.

Central tendency measures:

- Mean—the average
- Median—middle value
- Mode—value that occurs most often

Dispersion or distribution refers to the scattering of data around the central tendency. Its measures are:

- Range—the difference between the maximum and minimum values
- Variance—average squared deviation of each data point from the mean
- Standard deviation—square root of the variance

Types of data direct the type of analysis to be done:

- Continuous data can be measured to an infinite level, i.e., time, temperature, thickness.
- Categorical data falls into categories:
  - Ordinal—can be arranged into some natural order, i.e., short, medium, tall
  - Nominal—cannot be arranged into any natural order, i.e., colors, departments

At times, it may be necessary to collect data on a sample of the population rather than use data from the entire population. The purpose of sampling is to draw conclusions about the population using the sample. This is known as statistical inference.

Key considerations for sampling are:

- Sampling scheme: random, stratified
- Precision required ($\pm$?)
- Amount of characteristic's variation
- Confidence level (95%)
- Sample size

Qualities of a good sample include:

- Free from bias—bias is the presence or influence of any factor that causes the population or process being sampled to appear different from what it actually is.
- Representative—the data collected should accurately reflect a population or process. Representative sampling helps avoid biases specific to segments under
- investigation.
- Random—in a random sample, data is collected in no predetermined order, and each element has an equal chance of being selected for measurement. Random sampling helps avoid

Basic Statistics (continued)

biases specific to the time and order of data collection, operator, or data collector.

Benefit/Cost Analysis

Remedy Alternative	Manual	Computerized
One-time costs	$7,500	$134,000
Annual cost of one-time costs	$1,500	$26,800
Additional annual operating costs	0	$17,000
Annual cost savings	$1,462,200	$1,562,200
Net annual operating costs (savings)	($1,462,200)	($1,545,000)
Total annual costs (savings)	($1,460,500)	($1,518,200)
Problem impact	70%	75%
Customer satisfaction impact	Low	Low
Benefit/Cost Assessment Rank Team Average	**1.7**	**1.3**

Benefit/Cost Analysis

1. Estimate the one-time costs.
2. Estimate the additional annual operating costs.
3. Estimate the annual cost savings.
4. If possible, calculate how much of the problem is likely to be eliminated because of each proposed remedy. Otherwise, rank the impact of alternatives.
5. Assess the impact on customer satisfaction. Alternatives that reduce customer satisfaction should be discarded.
6. Calculate the net annual operating costs. A negative number means that net savings are expected.
7. Calculate annual costs of one-time costs.
8. Calculate total annual costs as the algebraic sum of net annual costs and the annual costs of one-time costs.
9. Review data and rank the alternatives.

Box Plots: Copier Repair Response Time

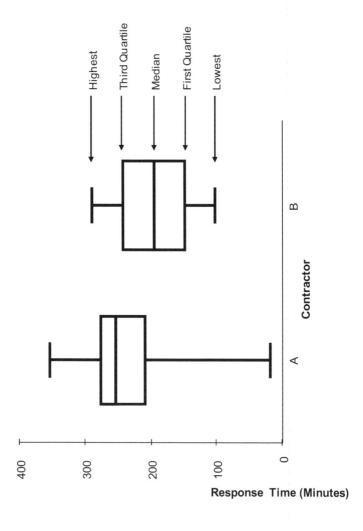

Box Plots

1. Collect the raw data and convert it to an ordered dataset by arranging the values from the lowest to the highest.
2. Decide on the type of box plot you wish to construct.
3. Calculate the appropriate summaries.
   Depth of the median =

   $$d(M) = \frac{n+1}{2}$$

   Depth of the first quartile =

   $$d(Q1) = \frac{n+1}{4}$$

   Depth of the third quartile =

   $$d(Q3) = \frac{3(n+1)}{4}$$

   Upper adjacent = the largest observation that is less the {Third Quartile + (1.5 x IQR)}
   Lower adjacent = the smallest observation that is greater than {First Quartile – (1.5 x IQR)}
4. Draw and label the horizontal axis.
5. Draw and label the vertical axis.
6. Draw the box plots.
   a. See the figure for the basic box plot.
   b. Use dashed whiskers for schematic box plots. The dashed whiskers should extend to the highest and lowest values in the dataset that are not outliers. These points are called adjacent values.
   c. Use asterisks to indicate all of the outliers on the schematic box plot.
7. Show a legend to define the parts of the box plot.
8. Title the chart and show the nominal values and limits (if applicable).
9. Analyze the pattern of variation.
10. Develop a plausible and relevant explanation for the pattern and determine your next steps.

Brainstorming

1. Prepare for brainstorming.
   a. Communicate the statement ahead of time.
   b. Provide appropriate materials (i.e. notecards, white-boards) for contributions.
2. Introduce the session.
   a. Review the conceptual rules.
      - No criticism or evaluation of any kind.
      - Be unconventional.
      - Aim for quantity of ideas in a short time.
      - "Hitchhike" on others' ideas.
   b. Review the practical rules.
      - Make contributions in turn.
      - Only one idea per turn.
      - You may pass.
      - Do not provide explanations.
3. Warm up.
4. Brainstorm.
   a. Write issue where it will be visible to all.
   b. Have another person write all contributions where visible.
   c. Stop before fatigue sets in.
5. Process ideas.

Calculating Sigma

1. Number of Units processed (N).
2. Number of Defect Opportunities Per Unit (O)
3. Total Number of Defects made (D)
4. Solve for Defects Per Opportunity (DPO)

$$DPO = \frac{D}{N \times O}$$

5. Convert DPO to Defects Per Million Opportunity (DPMO)

Look up process sigma in the Sigma Calculator toward the back of this book.

Let's assume you had 10,000 orders per year. Each of these orders then result in one invoice per order. We know that you have about a 10% error rate. So for every 10,000 orders there are 1,000 invoices with errors on them. There is also a chance each invoice could have one or more errors on them because there are at least 10 opportunities for errors on each invoice. Let's keep it simple. There are a total of 6680 errors (the 1000 invoices have an average of 6.68 errors per invoice). Running that number through the formula in step 4, we get .0668. Converting that number to DPMO (step 5), we get 66,800. Looking that up on our table, the $sigma_{st}$ equals 3.0 sigma.

Cause-Effect Diagram

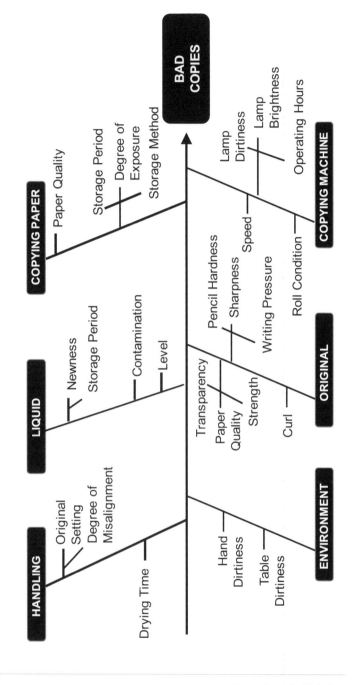

BAD COPIES

COPYING PAPER
- Paper Quality
- Storage Period
- Degree of Exposure
- Storage Method

LIQUID
- Newness
- Storage Period
- Contamination
- Level

HANDLING
- Original Setting
- Degree of Misalignment
- Drying Time

COPYING MACHINE
- Lamp Dirtiness
- Lamp Brightness
- Operating Hours
- Speed
- Roll Condition

ORIGINAL
- Pencil Hardness
- Sharpness
- Writing Pressure
- Transparency
- Paper Quality
- Strength
- Curl

ENVIRONMENT
- Hand Dirtiness
- Table Dirtiness

Cause-Effect Diagram

1. Define clearly the effect (the Y) for which the causes must be identified.
2. Place the effect or symptom being explained at the right, enclosed in a box. Draw the central spine as a thick line pointing to it.
3. Use brainstorming or a rational step-by-step approach to identify the possible causes (the Xs).
4. Each of the major areas of potential causes (not less than two and normally not more than five) should be placed in a box and connected with the central spine by a line at an angle of about 70 degrees.
5. Add potential causes for each main area, placing them on horizontal lines.
6. Add subsidiary causes for each cause already entered.
7. Continue adding possible causes until each branch reaches a potential root cause.
8. Check the logical validity of each causal chain. It should read "negative," i.e., a flat tire caused the car to swerve, a nail caused the tire to go flat, a person left a nail on the driveway.
9. Check for completeness.

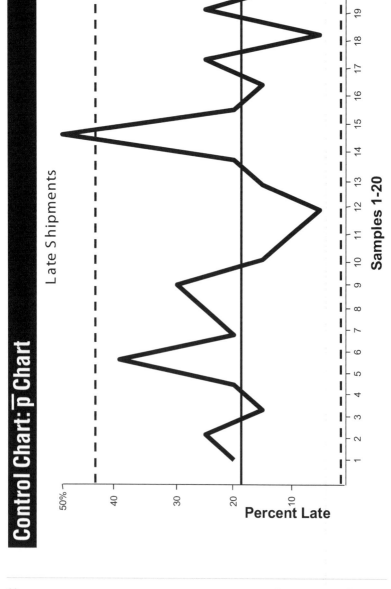

Late Shipments

UL

$\overline{x}$

LL

50%
40
30
20
10

Percent Late

Samples 1-20

1 2 3 4 5 6 7 8 9 10 11 12 13 14 15 16 17 18 19 20

Control Chart: p̄ Chart

The $\bar{p}$ chart is only one of many control charts.
1. Select control subject.
2. Establish measurement.
3. Measure the process at regular intervals.
4. Count total number of cases (**n**) and total number of defects for each point in time.
5. Calculate the percent defective.
6. Plot the percent defective (**p**).
7. Compute the average of **p** across the entire time period. This average is called **p-bar**, and it is indicated by the symbol $\bar{p}$.
8. Compute the standard deviation of $\bar{p}$.

$$s = \sqrt{\frac{\bar{p}(100\% - \bar{p})}{n}}$$

9. Compute the control limits.
   Upper Control Limit $= \bar{p} + 3 \times s$
   Lower Control Limit $= \bar{p} - 3 \times s$
10. Draw a horizontal center line indicating p-bar for each control limit. The control limit may be different at each point if "n" is different.
11. Remove points with assignable cause and recalculate control limits.
12. Regularly measure and plot the percent defective.
13. Take planned action on nonrandom variation.

Costs of Poor Quality (COPQ)

1. Identify the costs from processes that are non-value added. The result of this step is a list of all activities that contribute to poor quality because they exist only as the result of deficiencies occurring in the process. Each cost-of-poor-quality task identified, and indicates where in the organization the cost of each activity is measured, this is not necessarily where the error or deficiency occurs.
2. Estimate the costs for each activity based on a 12 month period.
   a. Total resources attributed to that deficiency
   b. Unit costs requires two pieces of data:
      – The number of times a particular deficiency occurs
      – The average cost for correcting and recovering from that deficiency when it does occur. This average cost, in turn, is computed from a list of the resources used to make the correction; the amount (units) used of each resource for a single correction; the cost of one unit of each resource.
   c. The cost of resources consumed for activities associated with costs of poor quality as a percent of total cost or total sales for the same 12-month period.
3. Group the cost into three categories:
   a. Inspection and appraisal
   b. Internal failures
   c. External failures
4. Collect the data and estimate the costs.
5. Analyze the results and decide on next steps.

This page has been intentionally left blank.

Customer Needs

Customer Needs \ Customers	Readers	Advertisers	Printers	Typesetters	Color separators	Newsstand
No last minute changes			●	●	●	
Material complete			●	●	●	
Enough complete			●	●	●	
It sells		●				●
Stable circulation		●				○
Catchy cover lines	○	●				●
Informative and well-written	●	○				○
Attractive	●	●				●

Legend

- ● Very strong relationship
- ○ Strong relationship
- △ Weak relationship

Customer Needs Spreadsheet:
Voice of the Customer (VOC)

1. Create a multi–column spreadsheet.
2. Label first column, "Customers." List, in priority order, the vital few customers. Include groups of "useful many" customers that, collectively, can be considered as vital few.
3. Label the top row, "Customer Needs," and list all discovered needs in the columns below. Enter one need for each column.
4. Correlate relationship between customers and needs.
   a. Create a legend to define the relationship.
   b. Base relationship on solid evidence.
   c. More than one customer can be addressed by the same need.
   d. Enter the appropriate value where needs and customers intersect.
   e. Review the spreadsheet and add any additional customers or needs that have been left off the list.
5. Go back and summarize the data you have collected.
6. Analyze each need in terms of:
   a. The strength of the relationship between needs and customers.
   b. The customer's importance.
7. Determine criteria and prioritize the needs from most critical to least critical.

Data Collection: An Overview

1. Formulate good questions that relate to specific information needs of the project.
2. Consider appropriate data analysis tools.
3. Define comprehensive data-collection points.
4. Select an unbiased collector.
5. Understand data collectors and their environment.
6. Design data-collection forms.
   a. Keep it simple.
   b. Reduce opportunities for error.
   c. Capture data for analysis, reference and trace ability.
   d. The form should be self-explanatory.
   e. The form must look professional.
7. Prepare the instructions.
8. Test forms and instructions.
9. Train data collectors.
10. Audit the collection process and validate the results. Place the product/features at the top and identify, in the far right column, the factors checked on the Critical Component Spreadsheet.

Design of Experiments (DOE)

DOE is a structured, organized method for determining the relationship between factors (Xs) affecting a process and the output of that process. DOE is an approach to collecting and analyzing data to determine:

- Effects of material variation
- Sources of variation
- Impact of the operator
- Cause-effect relationships between process inputs and product characteristics
- The equation which models your process

The formal plan for conducting the experiment is called the "experimental design" (or the "experimental pattern"). It includes the choices of the responses, factors, levels, blocks, and treatments and the use of certain tools called planned grouping, randomization, repetition and/or replication. Typically, the analysis of the results of an experiment is straightforward—particularly if computer-based tools, such as Minitab®, are available. It is the way in which we conduct the experiment that is key. The best analysis in the world cannot rescue a poorly designed experiment.

A factor (or input) is one of the controllable or uncontrollable variables whose influence on a response (output) is being studied in the experiment. A factor may be quantitative, e.g., temperature in degrees, time in seconds. A factor may also be qualitative, e.g., different machines, different operator, cleaned or not clean.

The "levels" of a factor are the values of the factor being studied in the experiment. Levels should be set wide enough apart that effects on the Y variable can be detected. For quantitative factors, each chosen value becomes a level, e.g., if the experiment is to be conducted at two different temperatures, then the factor of temperature has two "levels." A qualitative factor such as cleanliness can have two levels as well, particularly clean vs. not clean.

k1 x k2 x k3...Factorial: Description of the basic design. The number of "k's" is the number of factors. The value of each "k" is the number of levels of interest for that factor. Example: A 2 x 3 x 3 design indicates three input variables. One input has two levels and the other two each have three levels.

Failure Mode and Effect Analysis

Product: New Checking Account
Component: Printing New Checks

1	2	3	4	5	6	7	8	9
Mode of Failure	Cause of Failure	Effect of Failure	Frequency of Occurrence (1-10)	Degree of Severity (1-10)	Chance of Detection (1-10)	Risk Priority (1-1000) (4) x (5) x (6)	Design Action	Design Validation
Checks being printed incorrectly	Incorrect information on application form	Checks have to be re-issued	4	6	8	192	Clerk reviews information with customer	Clerk initials form after review
	Data entry error	Ditto	8	6	5	240	Review step in software	Run software
	Information entered in the wrong field on application	Ditto	5	6	2	60		

Note Following Assigned Values

Column/Value	1	2	3	4	5	6	7	8	9	10
4. Frequency (errors per 10,000 customers)	<2	4	8	10	15	20	25	30	35	<35
5. Severity for customer	Trivial				Cause Complaint			Major Time or $		Loss of customer
6. Detection	Certain				Possible					None

Failure Mode and Effect Analysis

1. Create a nine-column spreadsheet.
2. Create an assigned-values table.
3. In column 1, list all possible Modes of Failure. Each item should have a separate line.
4. In the next column, identify all possible causes of failure for each mode.
5. In column 3, determine the affect each failure will have on the customer, the overall product, other components, and the entire system.
   Note: For steps 6, 7, 8 use values established in assigned values table.
6. Evaluate the frequency of occurrence. Enter the appropriate integer in column 4.
7. Evaluate the degree of severity of each failure effect. Record appropriate value in column 5.
8. Evaluate the chance of detection for each cause of failure. Place this number in column 6.
9. Calculate the risk priority factor by multiplying columns 4, 5, and 6. Put the product in column 7.
10. Design action/remedy for only those "vital few" causes with the highest risk factors. Reduce the level of failure to a rate that is acceptable.
11. Validate each action/remedy.

Fault Tree Analysis

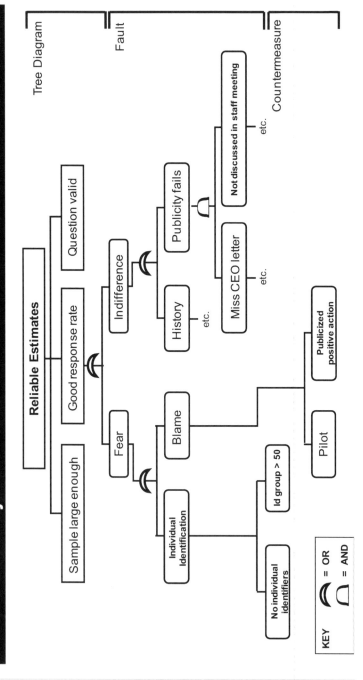

Fault Tree Analysis

1. Select a component that requires further analysis. Place component in a block at the top of diagram.
2. Under each block, identify the "faults" which will be analyzed (usually obtained from FMEA).
3. Underneath each fault, identify all causes for each. Causes are depicted by an oval and are connected to the appropriate fault. If a fault has several causes, each one should be represented.
4. Continue breaking down each cause until you have reached causes that can be controlled. Use:
   a. "And gates" whenever all faults listed below occur.
   b. "Or gates" whenever faults listed below have one or more cause occur.
5. Develop countermeasures for each cause. Label and graphically represent each one in a box placed under each specific cause.
   a. If any one factor alone from the two or more factors identified can cause failure, countermeasures must be designed for each.
   b. If two or more factors together cause failure, then only one factor needs countermeasures developed.
6. Repeat this activity for all critical failures.

Flow Diagram: Distribution of Technical Manuals

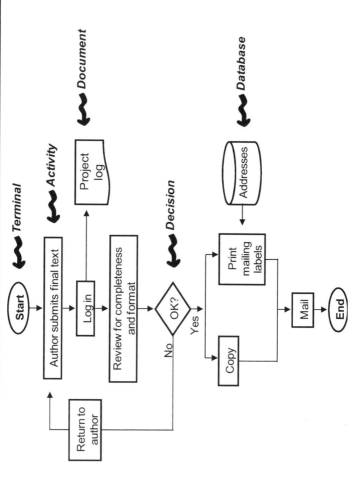

Flow Diagram/Process Map

1. Discuss how you intend to use the flow diagram or process map, and decide on the desired outcome of the session.
2. Define the boundaries of the process. Show the first and last steps, using appropriate flow diagram symbols.
3. Document each step in sequence, starting with the first (or last) step. Lay out the flow consistently from top to bottom or left to right.
4. When you encounter a decision or branch point, choose one branch and continue.
5. If you encounter an unfamiliar segment, make a note and continue.
6. Repeat steps 4, 5, and 6 until you reach the last (or first) step in the process.
7. Go back and flow diagram the other branches from the decision symbols.
8. Review the completed chart to see if you have missed any decision points or special cases.
9. Fill in unfamiliar segments and verify accuracy.
   a. Observe process.
   b. Interview knowledgeable people.
10. Analyze the flow diagram.

Glossary

1. Select a member of the team to act as Glossary Chief.
2. Use glossary worksheets to record each term and the unique meaning the team assigns to it.
3. Identify needs that must be translated. A need must be translated if there is any departure from unanimity on its meaning.
4. Choose a method for accomplishing translation.
    a. Translate by defining each term that has been identified as needing an interpretation or an explanation. Enter the terms along with their definitions on the glossary worksheet.
5. Identify other items such as:
    a. Product and process features
    b. Definitions and other issues related to testing:
        −   Modes of failures
        −   Critical factors
        −   Customer comments or comparative words
        −   Internal policy or procedural items
    c. Units of measures and sensors, etc.
6. Identify any samples to supplement the glossary. Enter them in your glossary and cross-reference it to the appropriate terms.

This page has been intentionally left blank.

Graphs and Charts

Sales Staff Time

PIE CHART

Labels: Administrative, With Customer, Travel, Training

Customer Complaints By Type

Jan-Apr 2001

Number of Defects

Legend:
- ▨ Cosmetic
- ☐ Dimensional
- ■ Electrical

Months: Jan, Feb, Mar, Apr — Month

BAR CHART

Operating Hours System Not Available

Hours

Months: Jan, Feb, Mar, Apr, May, June — Month

LINE CHART

Graphs and Charts

Line Graphs
1. Determine the range of the vertical axis and the size of each increment. Label the vertical axis.
2. Do the same for the horizontal axis.
3. Draw axes and, if needed, a grid.
4. Plot each data point.
5. Connect the points with a line.
6. Label and title the graph.

Bar Graphs
1. Determine the range of the vertical axis and the size of each increment. Label the vertical axis.
2. Choose a simple, grouped, or stacked bar graph.
3. Determine the number of bars. Draw the horizontal axis. Label the horizontal axis.
4. Determine the order of the bars.
5. Draw the bars.
6. Label and title the graph.

Pie Charts
1. Determine the percentage for each category.
2. Convert the percentage values into degrees.
3. Draw a circle with a compass and mark the segments of the pie chart with a protractor.
4. Label the segments and title the chart.

Histogram: Shapes and Interpretations

Bell-Shaped
natural, expected

Double-Peaked
two distinct processes

Plateau
many different processes

Comb
data errors

Skewed
*practical or
specification limit*

Truncated
forced removal; inspection

Isolated-Peaked
*two processes,
inefficient inspection*

Edge-Peaked
inaccurate data

Histogram

1. Determine the high value, low value and range.
    a. Range = high value – low value
2. Decide on the number of cells.

Data Points	Number of Cells*
20-50	6
51-100	7
101-200	8
201-500	9
501-1000	10
Over 1000	11-20

   *Less than 40 only as a result of stratification.
3. Calculate the approximate cell width.
    a. Approx. Cell Width = range / number of cells
4. Round the cell width to a convenient number.
5. Construct the cells by listing the cell boundaries.
6. Tally the number of data points in each cell.
7. Draw and label the horizontal axis.
8. Draw and label the vertical axis.
9. Draw bars to represent the number of data points in each cell.
10. Title chart and indicate total observations.
11. Identify and classify the pattern of variation.
12. Develop an explanation for the pattern.

Hypothesis Testing

Hypothesis testing refers to the process of using statistical analysis to determine if the observed differences between two or more samples are because of random change (as stated in the null hypothesis) or true differences in the samples (as stated in the alternate hypothesis). A null hypothesis (H_o) is a stated assumption that there is no difference in parameters (mean, variance, DPMO) for two or more populations. The alternate hypothesis (H_a) is a statement that the observed difference or relationship between two populations is real and not the result of chance or an error in sampling. Hypothesis testing is the process of using a variety of statistical tools to analyze data, and ultimately, to accept or reject the null hypothesis. From a practical point of view, finding statistical evidence that the null hypothesis is false allows you to reject the null hypothesis and accept the alternate hypothesis.

Hypothesis Testing Definitions

- Alpha Risk (α)—the maximum risk or probability of making a Type I Error. This probability is always greater than zero, and is usually established at 0.05.
- Alternative Hypothesis (H_a)—statement of change or difference. This statement is considered true if H_o is rejected.
- Beta Risk (β)—the risk or probability of making a Type II Error, or overlooking an effective solution to the problem.
- Confidence Level = $(1 - \alpha)$ 100%.
- Null Hypothesis (H_o)—This statement is assumed true until sufficient evidence is presented to reject it.
- Power = $(1 - \beta)$. The ability of a statistical test to detect a real difference or the probability of being correct in rejecting H_o. Commonly used to determine if sample sizes are sufficient to detect a difference in treatments if one exists.
- Significant Difference—the term used to describe the results of a statistical hypothesis test where a difference is too large to be reasonably attributed to chance.
- Test Statistic—a standardized value (z, t, F, etc.) which represents the feasibility of H_o, and is distributed in a known manner such that a probability for this observed value can be determined.
- Type I Error—the error in rejecting H_o when it is in fact true.
- Type II Error—the error in failing to reject H_o when it is in fact false, or in saying something is not statistically significant, when in fact, it is.

Kaizen

Kaizen is a Japanese word meaning improvement done without spending much money, which involves a cross section of personnel from managers to workers. Kaizen implies small improvements are made day after day, continuously.

Kanban

In a value stream, a Kanban is a signal; usually a 'card' authorizing production or delivery of required products or services, which is initiated by consumption from down-stream operations. Kanbans are used most often in the ordering of supplies because they keep costs low. Create a Kanban card for a product or service by the following steps:

1. Create minimum/maximum levels of products used in a designated time frame.
2. Create the Kanban Card; The Kanban Card should be large enough so that it is easily visible. Use colored paper and laminate the card if possible.
   The card should include:
   - Name and item number of the product or service
   - Minimum quantity
   - Maximum quantity
   - Standard re-order quantity
   - Suppliers name
3. Set up the Kanban Card and system. Place the Kanban Card on the re-order buffer stock.

Load Charts

In Lean, load charts are used to balance the process. Balancing (Heijunka) is the reallocation of resources (people and machinery) to accomplish a series of tasks with the goal of minimizing the idle time per resource for a given production volume and time period.

The following information is needed to construct a load chart:
- Sequence of tasks
- Total available working time
- Total customer demand
- Cycle time for each task

Use the following steps to construct a load chart:
1. Create a bar chart of each task on the same graph where the X-axis lists the sequence of process steps/tasks and the Y-axis displays the cycle time.
2. Calculate the takt time for the overall process and display on the same graph.
3. Adjust the sequence of steps by combining tasks and moving or adding additional workers per task until you can create a future state load chart.

Fixing the Measurement System

Measurement System Variation

Repeatability

- Poor Fixturing
- Excessive Within Part Variation
- Positioning of Gaps When Reading
- Maintenance Status of Gage
  - Gage not calibrated
  - Gage worn
- Environmental Conditions
  - Noise
  - Lighting
- Physical Conditions
  - Eyesight
  - Hearing
  - Resolution
  - Increments too large
  - Estimating required

Reproducibility

- Poor Fixturing
- Maintenance Status of Gage
  - Gage not calibrated
  - Gage worn
- Environmental Conditions
  - Noise
  - Lighting
- Physical Conditions
  - Eyesight
  - Hearing
  - Resolution
  - Increments too large
  - Estimating required

Stability

- New Operators
- Software Changes
- Gage
  - Warm-up time required
  - Plugged filters
- Manpower Conditions
  - Fatigue
  - New data collectors
- Environmental Conditions
  - Temperature variations
  - Humidity variations
  - Lighting
- Time Factors
  - Time of year, Time of day

Linearity

- Calibration
  - Gage not calibrated at high and low ends of scale
  - Worn high or low master
- Worn Gage

Accuracy

- Calibration
  - Gage not calibrated
  - Worn master
- Methods
  - Procedures unclear
  - Improper use

Measurement System Analysis (MSA)

The purpose of measurement system analysis (MSA) is to ensure and demonstrate that the measuring procedures and systems provide:

1. Adequate discrimination
2. Statistical stability over time
3. Proof that the measurement error (variation) is small relative to process variation and product/process requirements

MSA quantifies the amount of variation for:

- Accuracy
- Repeatability
- Reproducibility
- Stability
- Linearity

How to Complete an MSA Study:

- Complete the MSA Planning Worksheet to identify the question.
- Select the appropriate analysis tool.
- Collect data.
- Input the data and run the calculations.
- Analyze the data.
- Fix the measurement system (if necessary).

Multi-Vari Example

- Set up a graphical chart (Y-axis = response (output), X-axis = parts)
  - Add specifications to the chart (missing here)
  - Plot the "within" piece data points (or use max and min) for each part and connect with a vertical bar (Hint: the length of this bar represents positional variability)

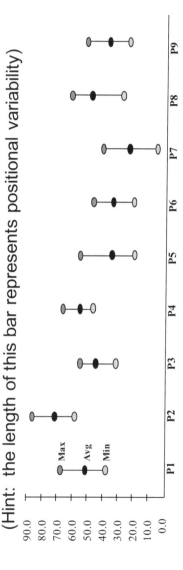

Multi-Vari Charts

A multi-vari chart is a tool that graphically displays patterns of variation. It is used to identify possible Xs or families of variation, such as variation within a subgroup, between subgroups, or over time. Each dot or symbol on the chart represents a specific data point. Each line represents the range of data for one subgroup.

A multi-vari chart allows you to see the effect multiple variables have on a Y. By looking at the patterns of variation, you can identify or eliminate possible Xs. This tool allows you to view the process in its natural state without introducing any artificial variation.

1. Look at how much the means vary from subgroup to subgroup, and estimate the amount of common cause variation by looking at the variation within the subgroups.

2. Special cause variation could be affecting your process if the means vary significantly from subgroup to subgroup. Answering the question of why the mean is shifting from subgroup to subgroup could lead you to the identification of an X.

3. Common cause variation could be greater than special cause variation if the variation within subgroups is greater than between subgroups. Answering the question of what is changing within the subgroup leads you to the identification of an X.

Pareto Analysis: Customer Complaints

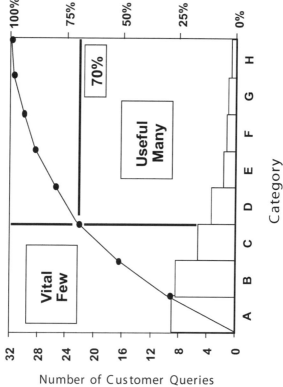

Pareto Analysis

1. Total the data on effect of each contributor and sum these to determine the grand total.
2. Re-order the contributors from the largest to the smallest.
3. Determine the cumulative-percent of total for each contributor.
4. Draw and label the left vertical axis from 0 to the grand total or just beyond.
5. Draw and label the horizontal axis. List the contributors from largest to smallest, going from left to right.
6. Draw and label the right vertical axis from 0 to 100%. Line up 100% with the grand total on the left axis.
7. Draw bars to represent the magnitude of each contributor's effect.
8. Draw a line graph to represent the cumulative-percent of total.
9. Analyze the diagram. Look for a break point on the cumulative-percent graph.
10. Title the chart; label the "vital few" and the "useful many."

Pay-Off Matrix

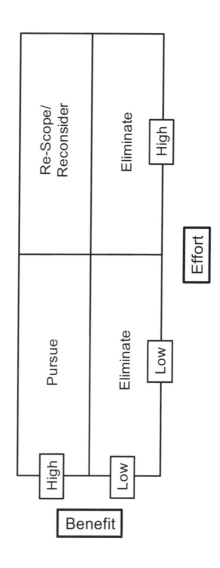

		Effort	
Benefit		Low	High
High		Pursue	Re-Scope/Reconsider
Low		Eliminate	Eliminate

Pay-Off Matrix

The pay-off matrix helps to evaluate and reduce the number of suggested solutions in terms of effort and benefit—the amount of effort necessary to implement a solution vs. the anticipated benefit achieved from implementing the solution.

Note: Before using the pay-off matrix, be sure all team members share the same operational definition of "high" and "low.

1. Draw a 2x2 grid on easel paper or a white board making sure that each box is large enough to contain sticky notes.
2. Using the bottom left corner as the origin, title the X-axis effort and the Y-axis benefit
3. Fill in the LOW and HIGH titles for the columns and rows. Make the LOWS closest to the origin, and the HIGHS farthest away. Follow the example on the previous page.
4. Now, after writing each solution on its own sticky note, and discuss as a team which quadrant to place each solution.
5. Focus first on the solutions that end up in the low-effort and high-benefit quadrant. Once complete, decide as a team if the high-effort, high-benefit should be addressed as well.

Planning Matrix and Tree Diagram

New Medical-Record Tracking Procedures

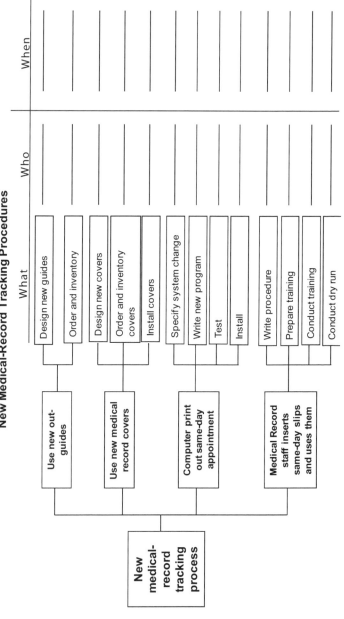

©2014 Juran Institute, Inc.

Planning Matrix and Tree Diagram

1. Use a tree diagram to identify all the tasks needed to complete a specific piece of work.
2. List each task on an adhesive note and post on the wall or flip chart in a vertical column.
3. Label other columns with "Who" and "When."
4. Work through the tasks one by one. Take the following steps:
   a. Discuss and identify the most appropriate person or group of persons to do the work.
   b. Agree on the necessary completion date.
5. Agree on how the team will monitor progress of the plan. Possibilities include the following:
   a. As an agenda item at each meeting, obtain a brief report on active tasks.
   b. Have the team leader (or a designated member) check with each responsible person before the meeting and enter on the agenda only those tasks that require discussion.
6. Transfer the matrix to standard paper and include it with future team minutes and agendas.

Planning Network

A planning network is a series of boxes connected by arrows. Each box indicates start and end dates for a single activity. An arrow from the right side of one activity to the left side of a second means that the second activity cannot start until the first one is complete. An arrow pointing to the middle of the box (as in the third activity below) means that it can begin, but not end, before the earlier activity ends.

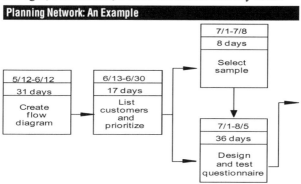

Planning Network: An Example

1. Generate and record all necessary tasks.
   a. Use Brainstorming or Tree Diagram.
   b. Record each task on a card or adhesive slip of paper.
      – Divide the card in half.
      – List task at the bottom.
2. Sequence all of the identified tasks.
   a. Create a "sequence flow" by placing task cards in rows based on their relationship to each other.
   b. Order goes from left to right beginning with the first necessary task.
   c. Lay out the row with the most tasks in a line.
   d. Organize the next longest path, etc.
   e. Determine simultaneous paths.
   f. Draw connections between the sequential paths.
3. Record time duration to each task or activity on top.
4. Calculate shortest implementation schedule.
   a. Find the path with longest total duration by adding up the total duration of each of the tasks along each path.
   b. Mark the path with the longest elapsed time using bold arrows. This is the critical path.
5. Calculate starting and finishing times for each task.
6. Validate the planning network and revise as needed.
7. Determine resources for each major task.

Probability

Probability, the formal study of the laws of chance, refers to the chance of something occurring, or the fraction of occurrence over a number of trials. Probability theory allots for dealing with uncertainty in a consistent and logical fashion.

Basic Definitions

- **Random Experiment:** The process of observing the outcome of a chance event. The outcome that occurs can't be predicted with certainty.
- **Elementary Outcome:** A possible result of the random experiment.
- **Sample Space:** The set or collection of all the elementary outcomes from the random experiment.
- **Simple Event:** The individual outcomes in a sample space.
- **Mutually Exclusive:** No two outcomes can occur simultaneously during one trial of the random experiment.
- **Random Variable:** A numerical outcome of a random experiment.
- **Probability Distribution:** The possible values of the random experiment and the probabilities connected with these values.

Determining Probability

- **Classical:** Based on gambling ideas that assume the game (experiment) is fair and all outcomes have the same chance of occurring.
- **Relative Frequency:** An experiment can be repeated and the event's probability is the proportion of times the event occurs in the long run.
- **Individual:** Most experiments are not equally likely or repeatable so the individual uses their personal opinion to assess the possible occurrence of the outcome.

Probability

- A probability distribution function is a mathematical formula that relates the numerical outcome of the random variable with their probability of occurrence.
- The collection of these probabilities is called a probability distribution.

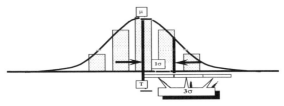

Process Capability

$$C_p = C_{pk} = 1.33$$

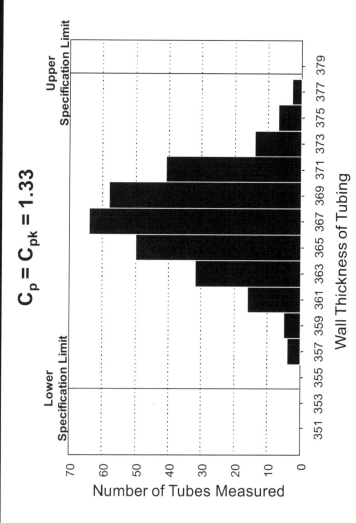

Process Capability

1. Identify the process subjects for measurement.
2. Establish units of measure, sensors, and upper and lower specification limits for the selected subjects.
3. Operate the process through a number of cycles. (A minimum of 40 observations without any assignable causes are usually needed.)
4. Identify and remove any observations that are out of control as the result of assignable causes.
5. Construct a histogram of the remaining observations for each subject.
6. Evaluate the process capability visually.
7. Calculate the C_{pk} index for each process subject.

$$C_{pk} = minimum \left\{ \frac{USL - \bar{x}}{3\sigma}, \frac{\bar{x} - LSL}{3\sigma} \right\}$$

   The index must, at a minimum, equal 1. 0. Most processes should have a minimum index of 1.33.
8. If the process is not capable, identify and eliminate the root causes for excessive variability.

Process Control Plan

Control Subject	Subject Goal	Unit of Measure	Sensor	Frequency of Measure	Sample Size	Criteria for Action	Action to be Taken	Location Assigned To
Spray delivery capacity	10 gallons per minute	Volume or flow per minute	Water meter	During start-up of every job	Each job	More than 11 Less than 9	Reduce flow speed Increase flow speed	On-site— worker
Crew size	One person per 10,000 sq. ft. of yard	# of workers per 10,000 sq. ft.	Foreman	During start of daily run - for each job and yard	Each job	Too many or too few call office	See Office Manager	On-site— foreman
Scheduling forecast on PC to determine to/from and work need	Forecast times always within 10% of actual	# of workers and location of job	Foreman	Every job	Weekly reports— total # of jobs per week	Compare actual #s of workers to est. # generated by program	Adjust program	Main office— traffic manager

Process Control Plan

1. Select possible control subjects.
2. Identify dominant variables for each subject.
3. Cluster subjects into different categories. Select the most critical variables to become the control subjects.
4. Create a multi-column spreadsheet.
5. Label column one, "Control Subjects." List subjects underneath using one row for each critical variable.
6. Label second column, "Subject Goal," and list the goal for each control subject.
7. Review a process map of your new process, and identify where to measure each control subject.
8. Outline a control plan for each control subject by listing those headings shown in the example.
9. Review the spreadsheet to verify that:
   a. All critical control subjects are identified
   b. The plan brings the process into control
   c. The plan makes maximum use of self-control and self-inspection

Process Load

Process load is the percent of available time required to run all products/services assigned to a given process step. It is calculated using changeover time (set up time), cycle time, rational batch sizes (RBS), annual demand, and total available time per year.

1. Calculate the Process Load by first determining the required time for each product/service run:
   Required Time = (RBS x cycle time) + Setup Time
2. Next, determine number of runs per year for each product:
   Runs per Year = Yearly Demand/RBS
3. Calculate required time to produce per year for each product/service:
   Required Time Per Year = Required Time x Runs Per Year
4. Calculate Process Load % :

$$\text{Process Load} = \frac{\sum(\text{Required time per year,all products}) \times 100}{\text{Available time per year}}$$

Product Quantity Analysis (PQ)

PQ analysis is a tool used to help identify and select value streams for improvement projects. It isolates the largest volume of products or services in both units and dollars. To conduct the analysis:

1. Start by creating a table with column headers for the type of product or service, the annual demand/quantity of units, the cost per unit, and the annual cost.

2. Perform Pareto Analysis on both the annual unit demand and the dollar quantities, paying close attention to the vital few of each.

3. Using the two Pareto charts or tables displaying the Pareto chart data, determine which product/services have both a high level of annual demand and annual cost. These select few product/services will provide good opportunities for improvement projects.

Product Routing Analysis (PR)

PR analysis, like PQ analysis is also used to help identify the value steams for improvement. However, PR looks at which parts or services are processed through similar steps/operations in the same sequence. Products going through these similar steps/operations are called "Product Families." PR can be used in two situations; 1) to validate PQ results and 2) substitute for PQ analysis if results from PQ are inconclusive.

To conduct the analysis:

1. Determine the vital few products or services from the PQ analysis.
2. Compare the routing/operations of each product or service to identify common processes.
3. Determine the Vital Few Product Families. These will become the value streams for process improvement.

This page has been intentionally left blank.

Pugh Matrix

Use this column to weigh the criteria in terms of importance.

Rate each alternative as better (+), worse (-), or same (S) at achieving criteria as compared to datum alternative.

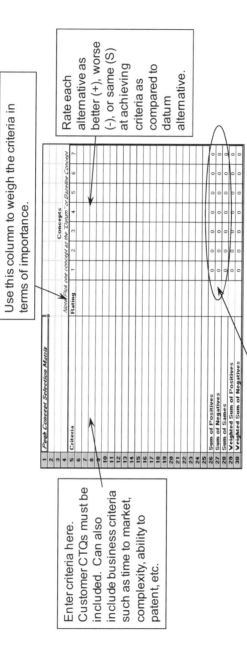

	Pugh Concept Selection Matrix								

Note: Pick one concept as the "Datum" or Baseline Concept

		Concepts							
	Criteria	Rating	1	2	3	4	5	6	7
6									
7									
8									
9									
10									
11									
12									
13									
14									
15									
16									
17									
18									
19									
20									
21									
22									
23									
24									
25									
26	Sum of Positives		0	0	0	0	0	0	0
27	Sum of Negatives		0	0	0	0	0	0	0
28	Sum of Sames		0	0	0	0	0	0	0
29	Weighted Sum of Positives		0	0	0	0	0	0	0
30	Weighted Sum of Negatives		0	0	0	0	0	0	0

Enter criteria here. Customer CTQs must be included. Can also include business criteria such as time to market, complexity, ability to patent, etc.

Compare the number of positives, negatives, and sames between alternatives. Can you create a new alternative that leverages the best of the initial alternatives?

Pugh Matrix

The Pugh Matrix is a useful tool for comparing several alternative concepts against pre-established criteria. It allows you to:

- Compare alternative solutions against project CTQs
- Create strong alternative solutions from weaker ones
- Arrive at an optimum solution that may be a hybrid or variant of the best of other solutions

Steps to construct a Pugh Matrix:

1. Enter the criteria. Customer CTQs must be included. Business criteria such as time to market, complexity, ability to patent, etc., can also be added.
2. Weigh the criteria in terms of importance.
3. Rate each alternative as better (+), worse (-), or same (s) at achieving criteria as compared to datum alternative.
4. Compare the number of positives, negatives, and sames between alternatives. Can you create a new alternative that leverages the best of the initial alternatives?

Push/Pull Systems

Push System

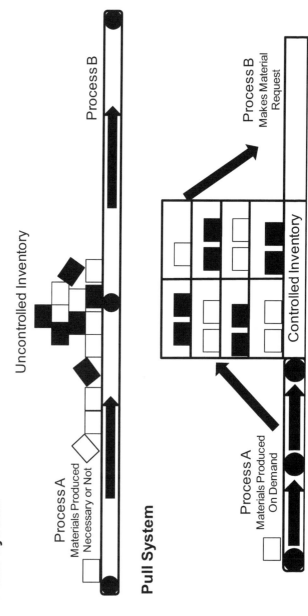

Uncontrolled Inventory

Process A
Materials Produced
Necessary or Not

Process B

Pull System

Process A
Materials Produced
On Demand

Controlled Inventory

Process B
Makes Material
Request

Push/Pull Systems

In traditional push systems, work (products or services) is delivered/ pushed downstream to the next operation or customer, based on a schedule without regard to the actual need of the work itself. This type of system creates excess inventory (product, information, patients, etc.) in the form of work-in-process and finished goods.

In a pull system, work is not delivered until it is needed by the downstream operation or customer. Pull controls the amount of inventory and triggers replenishment of a specified level of inventory based upon consumption or demand. Pull systems are created with the help of tools such as; Kanban, load charts, visual boards, standard work-in-process, etc.

Rapid Improvement Events

For these events, teams are focused on a topic for multiple days, typically 4 to 5. Teams are cross-functional from many parts of the business. Major team roles are team member, team leader, facilitator, and usually a consultant.

1. **2 to 3 Weeks Before the Event**
   a. Determine the target value stream.
   b. Create the team and charter.
   c. Determine key metrics and targets.
   d. Gather as much data as possible on:
      - Customer demand
      - Any backorders
      - Output from the process
      - Hours worked to create output
   e. Create productivity measures.

2. **1 to 2 Weeks Before the Event**
   a. Gather as much data as possible on same areas as before (above).
   b. Create productivity measures.
   c. Review for any problems, customer issues, scrap/rework issues, etc.
   d. Ensure team is ready and communicating.
   e. Ensure availability of equipment.

3. **1 Week Before the Event**
   a. Finalize boundaries of team.
   b. Confirm details (resources, logistics, food, timekeeping, supplies, schedule commitments, etc.)
   c. Train team members.
   d. Complete current state mapping.

4. **Day 1 of the Event**
   a. Validate value stream maps. (validate or complete "before values" for key metrics).
   b. Study current conditions.
   c. Make sure we understand the "before" values.
   d. Complete: VA/NVA decomposition analysis, current state load charts, floor space understanding, current state spaghetti diagrams, current state standard worksheets, etc.
   e. Review Day 1 and plan Day 2.

5. **Day 2 of the Event**
   a. Review results of Day 1.
   b. Review current state analysis.
   c. Design the future state.
   d. Design production control boards.
   e. Communicate, communicate.

Rapid Improvement Events (continued)

      f.   Develop future state standard work.

      g.   Begin to develop open issues ("To Do") List.

6. **Plan for Day 3**

    In implementing a future state, try to:

      a.   Specify a short time frame to institute and stabilize it.

      b.   Imagine how to remove wasted steps, flow remaining steps and customer pull.

      c.   Start mapping longer stretches of the value stream—downstream toward your customers; upstream toward your suppliers.

      d.   Start envisioning an "ideal state" in which all wasted steps have been removed and response time to the customer approaches zero—what technologies in what location will be necessary?

      e.   Review Day 2 activities.

      f.   Implement changes (big move).

      g.   Implement production control boards.

      h.   Make sure good parts are completed.

7. **Day 3 of the Event**

      a.   Review standard work, standard work-in-process, needed fixtures, to-do-list, etc.

      b.   Plan for Day 4.

8. **Day 4 of the Event**

      a.   Review Day 3 activities.

      b.   Analyze results on production control board.

      c.   MAIN GOAL OF TODAY—MAKE CELL SUCCESSFUL.

      d.   Review standard work, standard work-in-process, needed fixtures, to-do-list, etc.

      e.   Team helps and assists in keeping the cell on standard work and standard work-in-process.

      f.   Mark locations for standard work-in-process tools, fixtures, etc.

      g.   Plan for Day 5.

9. **Day 5 of the Event**

      a.   Review end of Day 4.

      b.   Prepare for presentation.

      c.   Present.

      d.   Review summary, accomplishments, and to-do list.

      e.   Acknowledge lessons learned.

Reliability Centered Maintenance (RCM)

Reliability Centered Maintenance allows an organization to move from reactive-failure based maintenance to a very proactive, predictive-condition based maintenance profile. It is based on intervals where there are known failure patterns, worn equipment parts, etc. Through analysis, maintenance requirements of an asset such as a machine or piece of equipment are defined and scheduled to improve reliability. By decreasing costly downtime when an asset unexpectedly fails, the efficiency and effectiveness of an overall process or system increases. The following questions help to analyze the asset:

1. What are the asset functions?
2. How can the functions fail?
3. What causes the functional failures?
4. What are the effects of each failure?
5. What are the consequences of each failure?
6. What can be done to prevent failures in the future?
7. If failure prevention can't be determined, what should be done?

RCM relies on a few key metrics to monitor equipment performance.

- Mean Time Between Failures (MTBF) refers to the average time that a piece of equipment runs until it fails.
- Mean Time to Repair (MTTR) refers to the average time from machine breakdown until the machine is repaired and able to be used again.
- Overall Equipment Effectiveness (OEE) refers to the product of the Machine Availability (MA) percent, the Machine Efficiency (ME) percent, and the Machine Quality (MQ) percent. It represents the cumulative effect of all losses because of equipment condition.

This page has been intentionally left blank.

Scatter Diagram: Common Patterns of Correlation

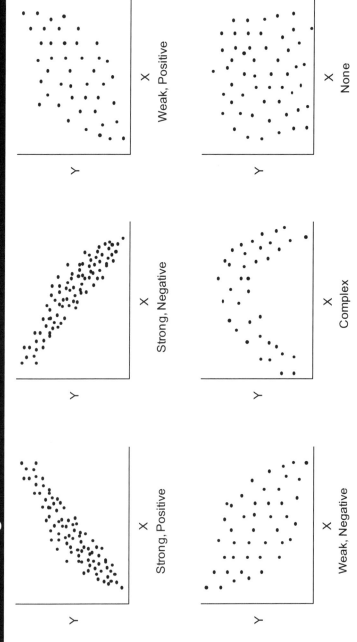

Scatter Diagram/Regression Analysis

1. Obtain table of paired data and determine the high and low values for each variable.
2. Put the suspected cause on the horizontal axis.
3. Draw and label the horizontal and vertical axes.
   a. Make the axes roughly the same length, creating a square plotting area.
   b. Label the axes in about six convenient multiples of 1, 2, or 5.
   c. Label increasing values from bottom to top and left to right.
   d. Provide a caption to describe the measurement and units.
4. Plot the paired data.
   a. Use concentric circles to indicate identical paired-data points.
   b. Use filled and unfilled symbols to show the strata.
5. Title the chart and label.
6. Identify and classify the pattern of correlation.
7. Check for potential pitfalls in your analysis. Consider confounding factors and other possible explanations for the correlation pattern.

Sigma$_{ST}$ Calculation Table

SIX SIGMA TABLE
(Defects/Millions are rounded)

% Defective	DPMO	Process Sigma	Yield
0.00034	3.4	6.0	99.99966%
0.0005	5	5.9	99.9995%
0.0008	8	5.8	99.9992%
0.001	10	5.7	99.9990%
0.002	20	5.6	99.9980%
0.003	30	5.5	99.9970%
0.004	40	5.4	99.9960%
0.007	70	5.3	99.9930%
0.01	100	5.2	99.9900%
0.015	150	5.1	99.9850%
0.023	230	5.0	99.9770%
0.033	330	4.9	99.9670%
0.048	480	4.8	99.9520%
0.068	680	4.7	99.9320%
0.096	960	4.6	99.9040%
0.135	1,350	4.5	99.8650%
0.186	1,860	4.4	99.8140%
0.255	2,550	4.3	99.7450%
0.346	3,460	4.2	99.6540%
0.466	4,660	4.1	99.5340%
0.621	6,210	4.0	99.3790%
0.819	8,190	3.9	99.1810%
1.07	10,700	3.8	98.930%
1.39	13,900	3.7	98.610%
1.78	17,800	3.6	98.220%
2.27	22,700	3.5	97.730%
2.87	28,700	3.4	97.130%
3.59	35,900	3.3	96.410%
4.46	44,600	3.2	95.540%
5.48	54,800	3.1	94.520%
6.68	66,800	3.0	93.320%

SIX SIGMA TABLE
(Defects/Millions are rounded)

% Defective	DPMO	Process Sigma	Yield
8.08	80,800	2.9	91.920%
9.68	96,800	2.8	90.320%
11.5	115,000	2.7	88.50%
13.5	135,000	2.6	86.50%
15.8	158,000	2.5	84.20%
18.4	184,000	2.4	81.60%
21.2	212,000	2.3	78.80%
24.2	242,000	2.2	75.80%
27.4	274,000	2.1	72.60%
30.8	308,000	2.0	69.20%
34.4	344,000	1.9	65.60%
38.2	382,000	1.8	61.80%
42	420,000	1.7	58.00%
46	460,000	1.6	54.00%
50	500,000	1.5	50%
54	540,000	1.4	46%
57	570,000	1.3	43%
61	610,000	1.2	39%
65	650,000	1.1	35%
69	690,000	1.0	31%

1. Select a typical process or transaction in which you are involved. For example, the billing process.
2. Estimate how many possible opportunities for defects there are in each transaction.
   * Example: 50 fields on each invoice
3. Calculate the current (estimate) defect rate which is the average number of defects per transaction.
   * Example: for every 4 invoices, there are 3 defects

$$\frac{3 \text{ defects}}{4 \text{ forms} \times 50 \text{ fields}} = \frac{3}{200} = .015 \text{ defect rate}$$

This is the same as 1.5 defects per 100 or 15,000 per 1,000,000 opportunities.
4. Determine your sigma level using the table above with either column for defects per 100 or defects per 1,000,000.

*NOTE: Defects per 1,000,000 are rounded numbers and we are assuming one-sided spec limits.

Single Minute Exchange of Dies (SMED)

SMED is a set of techniques to perform equipment setup and changeover operations in less than 10 minutes. It was originally developed for die presses, but the principle applies to all types of changeovers from preparing a machine for an alternate operation to preparing the Operating Room in a hospital for the next arriving patient. Decreasing the changeover times of an operation allows more flexibility and smaller batch runs. SMED helps to decrease the build-up of inventory or products/services which occur when a process runs for long time periods to "absorb" the cost of setup. SMED also helps improve capacity, throughput, and on-time delivery to the customer.

SIPOC

Supplier	**I**nput	**P**rocess	**O**utput	**C**ustomer	**C**TQs
Groups	Quote sheet	Determine if new or renewal	Groups installed on HPI Plan	Insured	Determine correct group
Sales	Rate sheet	Benefits underwriter triggers internal review	Rates verified	Members	Correct rate
Underwriting	Paperwork checklist	Rates verified	Billing occurs	Sales	Correct rate paid

SIPOC

SIPOC stands for supplier, input, process, output, and customer. It's a high-level map showing a process's supplier, the inputs received from them, and the process that adds value to those inputs. That process produces an output that meets or exceeds customer requirements. This model is applicable to both product and service processes. Everyone takes inputs from suppliers, adds value through their processing steps, and provides an output or outputs that, at a minimum, meet the customer's needs (CTQs).

1. Define the process, name it, and define the start and stop points.
2. Identify suppliers and the critical inputs the process receives from them.
3. Identify the customers of the process (those who receive the outputs) and the outputs of the process that respond to customer needs.
4. Identify the 5 – 8 major process steps that produce the output.
5. Validate the process map by working with the key functions that perform the major steps.

As you move through the DMAIC phases, you will use detailed process maps and value stream maps. See those sections in this guide.

SMART Method

An effective goal statement has five characteristics. These are captured in the term SMART, an acronym for the aspects of a goal that are most likely to provide focus and create commitment.

Criteria

1. Goals should be **S**pecific—cover the what, when, and how of a situation.
2. Goals should be **M**easurable—cover areas such as quantity, quality, costs, and/or time.
3. Goals should be **A**greed Upon—agreement that the end result is desirable and achievable.
4. Goals should be **R**ealistic—cover areas such as practicality, available resources, control over variables and authority.
5. Goals should be **T**ime-phased—completed within the needed time frame.

This page has been intentionally left blank.

Solution/Selection Matrix

Criterion	Weight	Alternative 1	Alternative 2	Alternative 3
Remedy Name		Overhaul and change speed	Replace equipment	Retain and change speed
Total cost	20	5	2	4
Impact on the problem	10	3	5	4
Benefit and cost relationship	30	4	3	5
Cultural impact and resistance to change	20	4	5	1
Implementation time	2	5	4	2
Uncertainty about effectiveness	6	4	5	3
Health and safety	10	4	5	5
Environment	2	3	3	3
Average Rating		**4.10**	**3.74**	**3.68**

Solution/Selection Matrix

1. Agree on the criteria to be used to evaluate the alternatives.
2. Each team member allocates a total of 100 points among the criteria.
3. Calculate the average number of points allocated to each criterion.
4. Review and agree on the weights.
5. Assemble the list of alternatives to be evaluated.
6. Rate each alternative. Each team member rates each alternative according to how well it meets each criterion, using a scale of 1 (worst possible) to 5 (best possible).
7. Calculate each team member's average rating for each alternative.
8. Give each team member a table showing how each member rated each alternative.
9. Discuss the ratings and reach consensus on the next steps.

This matrix can be used to select projects and, as in this example, to select solutions.

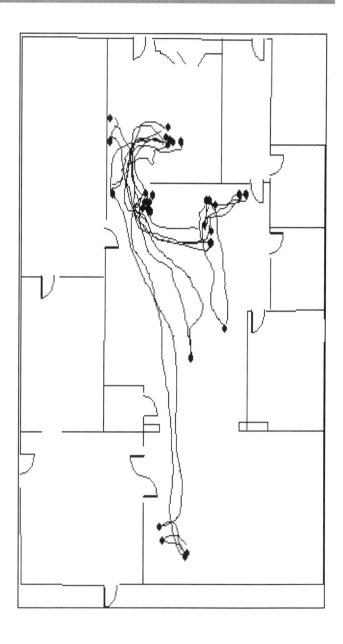

Spaghetti Diagram

Spaghetti Diagram

A spaghetti diagram is a facility layout showing the processing path of a product or service. This tool is used both in developing current state and future state value stream maps.

Step 1: Either draw the bird's eye view of the area where the value stream takes place or use an already existing blue print.

Step 2: Follow an employee or a product from the beginning of the process to the end, tracing the direction of movement throughout the facility layout.

Standard Work

A tool used to clearly define the roles and responsibilities of an operator while performing an operation. Standard work helps to eliminate inconsistencies between operators which can ultimately produce errors and defects in a process.

A Standard work form generally:
- Details the motion of the operator and the sequence of action
- Provides a routine for consistency of an operation
- Provides a basis for improvement
- Details the best process currently known and understood

This page has been intentionally left blank.

128B PIN PROBLEM

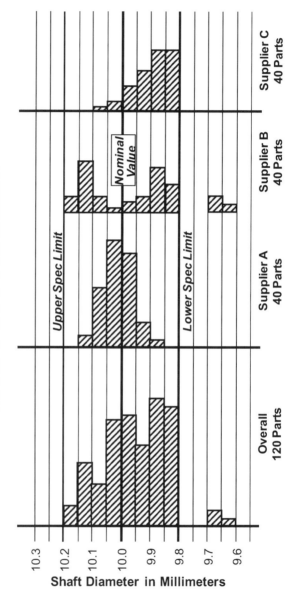

Stratification

1. Select the stratification variables. If new data are to be collected, be certain that all potential stratification variables are collected as identifiers.
2. Establish categories that are to be used for each stratification variable. The categories may be either discrete values or ranges of values.
3. Sort observations into the categories of one of the stratification variables. Each category will have a list of the observations that belong to it.
4. Calculate the phenomenon being measured for each category. These calculations can be a count of the number of observations in the category, an average value for those observations, or a display (like a histogram) for each category.
5. Display the results. Bar graphs are usually the most effective.
6. Prepare and display the results for other stratification variables. Repeat steps 2 through 5. Do second-stage stratification as appropriate.
7. Plan for additional confirmation.

Takt Time

The phrase takt time is from the German word for meter, as in music, which establishes the pace, or beat of the music. It is the time which reflects the rate at which customers buy one unit.

$$\text{Takt Time} = \frac{\text{available time (in a day)}}{\text{average daily demand}}$$

Available time includes such things as:
- Scheduled work time
- Consistently scheduled overtime
- Unscheduled, infrequent time for meetings, etc.

It does not include:
- Scheduled breaks
- Scheduled lunch
- Scheduled downtime (PM, plant shut-downs, clean-up)
- Regularly scheduled meetings (shift change, team meetings)

Practical takt time may need to be modified depending on variability of the process. When modifying takt time beyond the simple equation, another name should be used, such as cell takt or machine takt. Although modifiers may be planned, they are still waste (planned waste).

Takt Rules

Annual Demand	Approximate Takt Time
1 million	20 seconds
300 thousand	1 minute
100 thousand	3 minutes
50 thousand	6 minutes
10 thousand	30 minutes
5 thousand	1 hour
1 thousand	5 hours

To determine manpower or staffing:

$$\frac{\text{Total Labor Time in Process}}{\text{Takt Time}} = X$$

Total Productive Maintenance (TPM)

The origins of TPM are in the expansion of maintenance into a more comprehensive view with increased employee involvement. Equipment maintenance was formerly carried out by the operation. After work became more organized and specialized, preventive maintenance was turned over to specialists. This was typically a small group of highly trained individuals who could fix nearly any problem with the machine. TPM is a philosophy of manufacturing that focuses on the effective relationship of workers to equipment and the meaning and elimination of waste.

Routine maintenance responsibilities are carried out by all employees through small group activities so troubles are identified by the employee before quality begins to suffer.

TPM involves:

- Preventive Maintenance: Routine inspections, replacements, and repairs on a scheduled basis.
- Corrective Maintenance: Redesigning and/or modifying equipment to prevent breakdowns or simplify maintenance.
- Breakdown Maintenance: A plan enabling quick response to unscheduled breakdowns.
- Maintenance Prevention: Installing equipment that needs little maintenance.

TPM is a valuable tool when inspecting your facility and the following are found:

- Dirty equipment
- Leaks
- Buildup of raw material waste
- Tangled lines (electrical, pneumatic, hydraulic)
- Dismantling of equipment for inspections
- Clutter

Value Analysis

Product: Store Front Pre-Natal Clinic

Customer Need (listed in priority order)	Product Feature and Goals						Cost of Meeting Need
	Walk in appointments handled by Nurse, 5 days a week	Board Certified Obstetrician, 2 days a week	Social Worker, 5 days a week	Nutritional Counselor, 5 days a week	On-site Billing Clerk takes Medicaid insurance from all eligible patients	On-site laboratory - most results under 1 hour	
Convenient to use	60,000	30,000	10,000	10,000	20,000	40,000	170,000
Confidence in staff		70,000	10,000	15,000			95,000
Reasonable cost						25,000	25,000
Sensitivity			15,000	5,000			20,000
Informed choice			5,000	15,000			20,000
Cost for Feature	60,000	100,000	40,000	45,000	20,000	65,000	330,000

Value Analysis

1. Rank customers' needs based on their priorities.
2. Create a multi-column matrix.
3. Label the first column, "Customers' Needs." List them, in priority order, using one row for each need.
4. Label the top row of the matrix, "Product Features and Goals." Enter one feature and related goal for each column in priority order.
5. Label the far right column, "Cost of Meeting Needs." Also, label the bottom row, "Cost for Feature."
6. Enter the total cost for producing each product feature at the bottom of the corresponding column.
7. Allocate each feature's total cost to the customer's needs. Be sure all columns add up to the totals.
8. Sum all costs in each row and enter the total.
9. Check that the sum of all rows in the "Cost of Meeting Needs" column equals the total of the feature columns at the bottom of the last row.
10. Compare the results and consider changes to the design based on the analysis.
11. Using costs marked up to selling price, ask the customer whether they would pay the incremental costs for feature to meet needs.
12. Develop alternative designs based on feedback.

Value Stream

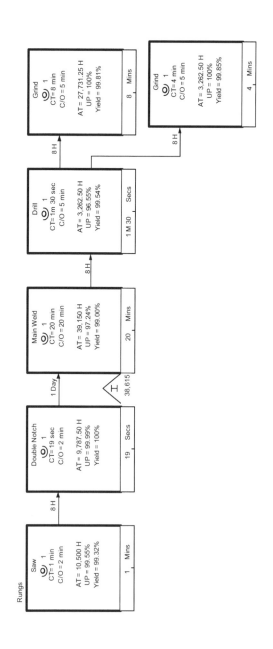

Rungs

Saw
1
CT= 1 min
C/O = 2 min

AT = 10,500 H
UP= 99.55%
Yield = 99.32%

1 | Mins

8 H

Double Notch
1
CT= 19 sec
C/O = 2 min

AT = 9,787.50 H
UP= 99.99%
Yield = 100%

19 | Secs

1 Day

38,615

Main Weld
1
CT= 20 min
C/O = 20 min

AT = 39,150 H
UP= 97.24%
Yield = 99.00%

20 | Mins

8 H

Drill
1
CT= 1m 30 sec
C/O = 5 min

AT = 3,262.50 H
UP= 96.55%
Yield = 99.54%

1 M 30 | Secs

8 H

Grind
1
CT= 8 min
C/O = 5 min

AT = 27,731.25 H
UP= 100%
Yield = 99.81%

8 | Mins

8 H

Grind
1
CT= 4 min
C/O = 5 min

AT = 3,262.50 H
UP= 100%
Yield = 99.85%

4 | Mins

Value Stream

- Is a powerful tool for analyzing information and flow throughout or between organizations in order to identify and plan improvements.
- Provides the clarity to reduce inventory and improve lead time, and plan and identify lean rapid improvement events for optimum effectiveness.
- Allows participants from different parts of an organization to gain an understanding of the overall information and material flow.
- Making breakthrough improvement requires out-of-the-box, cross-functional thinking. You must be able to see the waste across the entire flow of work to gain the clarity to eliminate it.
- Value stream mapping is a tool to help you visualize your current state in order to realize the future state.

Value Stream Mapping

Is a method for constructing a visual representation of a value stream. These maps outline information flow and product or service flow in both the "current state" (how the process operates in the present) and "future state" (how the process will operate after improvements).

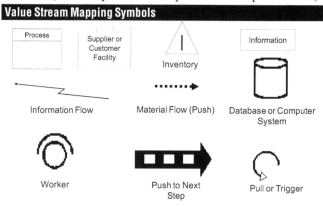

Value Stream Mapping Symbols

Process

Supplier or Customer Facility

Inventory

Information

Information Flow

Material Flow (Push)

Database or Computer System

Worker

Push to Next Step

Pull or Trigger

Visual Control Boards

Visual Control Boards are devices intentionally designed to share information at a glance to all employees—without having to say a word. There are many different types of boards used for various processes and functions.

A simple example is a wall board in a hospital listing Nurses and Physicians scheduled for the shift and the rooms they are assigned to. In manufacturing, shadow boards (boards with either a shadow or label of the tool that should be returned and stored on the board after every use) may be used to quickly identify missing tools and equipment.

Andon boards are used to visually notify employees that an error has occurred in the operation and the process should be shut down to fix the issue.

Production control boards are used to visually communicate production pace against plan, quality and maintenance issues, and problem resolution activities so all are aware of the current production status.

This page has been intentionally left blank.

JURAN® GLOBAL

Lean & Six Sigma

Reference Guide & Tool Kit

Team Skills

1. Building Rapport
2. Effective Meetings
3. Giving Feedback
4. Listening Techniques
5. Making Team Decisions
6. Multivoting
7. Negotiating Differences
8. Nominal Group Technique
9. Preparing Presentations
10. Providing Information
11. Questioning Techniques
12. Team Interactions

Building Rapport

1. To build rapport:
   a. Use common courtesy.
   b. Make a personal connection, such as sharing your own experience that was similar to the point being discussed.
   c. Use team language, such as we, our, let's, together, and we can.
   d. Display positive facial and body language, such as nodding, frequent eye contact, and smiling.
   e. Acknowledge that you hear and understand other people's points of view, even when you do not agree with them.
2. Avoid undermining rapport with:
   a. Rudeness
   b. Inappropriate tone of voice, such as curtness or condescension
   c. Inaccuracy
   d. Demanding jargon, such as "you must" or "we must"
   e. Technical jargon

Effective Meetings

1. Establish meeting guidelines.
   a. Brainstorm possibilities.
   b. Select guidelines.
   c. Provide copies for all members.
2. Plan the meeting.
   a. Set objectives—specific, observable results.
   b. Handle logistics.
   c. Prepare the agenda.
3. Conduct the meeting.
   a. Open the meeting.
      - Explain the purpose of the meeting.
      - Describe how the purpose will be achieved.
   b. Close the meeting.
      - Summarize the results.
      - Confirm the next steps and responsibilities.
4. Evaluate the meeting.
   a. General evaluation
   b. Focused evaluation form
5. Prepare meeting documents.
   a. Meeting minutes
   b. Reports
   c. Project log
   d. Storyboard

Giving Feedback

1. Positive Feedback. Use when a person:
    a. Exceeds performance expectations
    b. Consistently meets performance expectations
    c. Demonstrates improvement
    d. Shows a willingness to contribute or add value
    To use:
    -   Give specific examples of what you would like repeated
    -   Describe the benefits
2. Constructive feedback. Use when:
    a. Evaluating theories, alternatives, options, suggestions, ideas, etc.
    b. Identifying an error
    To use:
    -   State the positives—what you like about a contribution
    -   State the disadvantages—what you do not like
    -   Avoid joining the two parts with words like "but"
    -   Describe the reasons—why you do not like it

Listening Techniques

1. Affirm with words like:
   a. "Really?"
   b. "Uh-huh"
   c. "I see"
   d. "Sure"
2. Bridge by tying what the speaker just said to some related part of the topic. Examples include:
   a. "As you mentioned earlier . . ."
   b. "That reminds me to ask you. . . "
   c. "I'd like to follow up on. . ."
3. Organize and listen:
   a. Put unrelated materials aside.
   b. Sit in a location comfortable for listening.
   c. Arrange to avoid interruptions.
4. Confirm.
   a. State what you understood.
   b. Check that the statement is correct. For example:
      - "Is that correct?"
      - "Is that it?"
      - "Right?"

Making Team Decisions

There are three general types of decisions:
1. Data-driven decisions
2. Decisions by an authority
3. Decisions by consensus

A team reaches consensus when all team members can support a particular choice. Some members may not favor the choice, but they can proceed on the basis of that choice and will not oppose it.

Consensus is not:
- Agreement by all
- Majority vote
- Complete satisfaction by everyone

To reach consensus:
- State the proposed team decision simply
- Ask the team whether that is their understanding and whether they can support it
- If all agree and support the statement, declare that consensus has been reached

Multivoting

1. Generate a list of ideas.
2. Combine options that are agreed to be the same.
3. Number options sequentially on a master list.
4. Each team member has a specified number of votes, which is set equal to approximately one-third the total number of options on the list.
5. Tally the votes for each option on the master list.
6. Eliminate options with fewest votes.

Number of participants	Eliminate option with
4 or 5	1 or 2 votes
6 or 7	3 or fewer votes
8 or more	Votes from fewer than half the participants

7. Repeat steps 3 through 6 until the desired number of options remain.
8. Discuss the results and decide on the next steps.

Negotiating Differences

1. **Define the difference.**
   a. State what is important to you.
   b. Use clarifying and confirming words/phrases to state what is important to the other person.
2. **Explore alternatives.**
   a. Invite suggestions from others on how to resolve the difference.
   b. Offer your own suggestions.
   c. Provide both positive and constructive feedback on suggestions.
3. **Confirm agreed next steps.**
   a. Once you believe agreement has been reached, it is crucial to confirm your understanding of the next steps to be taken. This ensures that there is no misunderstanding and it increases the commitment of all to the final result.

Nominal Group Technique

Part 1

1. Define the topic so that it is specific and unbiased.
2. Describe the process to be followed. (See "Brainstorming" for rules, except that contributions are read in turn.)
3. Write the question where all can see.
4. Write down the ideas individually. Set a time limit usually 15 minutes.
5. Write all the ideas on a master list, reading ideas in turn.
6. Clarify and combine like ideas.

Part 2

1. Reduce master list to 50 using multivoting and renumber.
2. Distribute ballots to each team member as follows:

Number of ideas remaining on master list	Number of ballots to each team member
20 or fewer	4
12 to 25	5
26 to 35	6
36 to 40	7
40 or more	8

Preparing Presentations

1. Identify the objectives.
   a. What is the presentation supposed to accomplish?
   b. Who needs to be in the audience to meet objectives?
2. Anticipate the needs of the audience, such as:
   a. Information
   b. Clarification
   c. Assurance of progress
   d. Assurance of effectiveness
3. Assemble supporting data and information according to the DMAIC steps.
4. Develop the presentation. A presentation has three distinct phases.
   a. Introduction
   b. Body, with a few main points:
      – Identify the source of information
      – Provide information to support each point
      – Avoid unnecessary information
      – Avoid unfamiliar jargon
      – Use pictures of data, not words
   c. Conclusion
5. Create visual-aid support.

Providing Information

1. Preparation
   a. Identify the purpose for presenting the information.
   b. Anticipate the audience's needs and questions.
   c. Outline the information to achieve the purpose and meet the audience's needs.
2. Delivery
   a. Set the stage.
      - Identify the purpose of the discussion.
      - Capture interest with one important highlight.
   b. Present information.
      - Make sure that the information is clear, complete, and accurate.
      - Avoid unnecessary technical language and details.
      - Avoid unnecessary information.
      - Avoid unfamiliar jargon.
   c. Confirm understanding.
      - Ask open-ended questions.

Questioning Techniques

1. **Open-Ended Questions**
   Use when you need broad, general information; are uncertain about the topic; want a sense of feeling or attitudes; need elaboration on a topic.

2. **Closed-Ended Questions**
   Use when you want specific information; need to control a long-winded speaker; want a specific detail; want to confirm a person's commitment or agreement; are not clear about the meaning or significance of something; need to narrow down alternatives.

   Closed-ended questions usually begin with phrases like:
   a. "How often?"
   b. "How many?"
   c. "Who?"
   d. "When?"
   e. "Where?"

3. **Clarifying Questions**
   Use when you do not have enough information or when you do not understand what was said.

   To use:
   a. Ask a question about what has been said
   b. Ask why it was said

4. **Confirming Questions**
   Use when you want to ensure you understand what was said or when your immediate reaction is to reject, ignore, or disagree with what was said.

   To use:
   1. State what you understood, in your own words
   2. Check that your statement is correct. For example:
      - "Is that correct?"
      - "Is that it?"
      - "Right?"

Team Interactions

1. **No-response situations.** Summarize. Invite specific responses. Use questions likely to be answered.
2. **Overly talkative team member.** Summarize or ask for summary. Invite other responses. Set time limits.
3. **Quiet team member.** Ask direct personal questions. Summarize and clarify often. Use facial expressions to invite responses. Use written responses.
4. **Irrelevant issues.** Point out irrelevance. Point out when it would be relevant.
5. **Side conversations.** Ignore. Ask to share. Take a break.
6. **Disagreement among team members.** Confirm understanding. Ask factual questions. Apply "Negotiating Differences."
7. **Fear of rejection.** Confirm suggestion and appreciation. Ask for reasons for rejection. Ask for other suggestions.
8. **Senior team member.** Have senior members go last. Write down individual suggestions.

Made in the USA
San Bernardino, CA
10 October 2014